Easy Italian FAVORITES

Compiled by
**Professional Home Economics Teachers
of California, Nevada, Arizona and Utah**

Editor
Gerry Murry Henderson

Graphic Design, Typography and Production
Mike Burk Production Services, Long Beach, CA

Library of Congress Catalog
Card No. 83-072754
ISBN 0-914159-16-X

*A*merica has many "favorite foods", and always right up there at the top are "Italian Favorites"… the very sound of those words brings thoughts of family, warmth, relaxation, and good food!

For over twenty years, now, California Cookbook Company has been closely associated with Home Economics Teachers who help us publish a different book each year. We are proud to be associated with them, and wish you *buon appetito* as you enjoy over 300 of their recipes presented in this book!

Many people contribute to the production and distribution of our books each year:

- Nancy Freeman, our CCC Office Manager, is the first to receive each recipe, proof it, and input it into our computer. **THANK YOU,** Nancy, for eight great years!

- Gerry Henderson, of Temple City High School, a Certified Home Economist, edits each and every recipe, and makes sure "it's right"!

- Doug Herrema, of Huntington Beach, plans a year ahead each publication and finds appropriate photography.

- Doug Pierce, of Los Angeles, who works a more expanded area than any of us, was convinced that it was "high time" for an Italian publication!

- Mike Burk, of Long Beach, creatively designs and "packages" the entire book, the covers, photos, and art work.

- Jerry Bernstein, of KNI, Inc., in Anaheim, is a consummate professional in the world of printing, and has handled our publications over ten years now.

- "Rich" Richardson, Bill Horton, George Goyich, and Roger Uppermann, each drive long distances to distribute these books to schools and students who are selling them.

- Generous foods companies and councils contribute the beautiful photos within the book: Borden Foods of Columbus, OH; Lawry's Foods of Monrovia, CA; American Sheep Industry of Engelwood, CO; National Cattleman's Beef Association of Chicago, IL; Wisconsin Milk Marketing Board of Madison, WI; and the Pillsbury Company of Minneapolis, MN.

- And a **GREAT BIG THANK YOU** to the students who sell our books in the schools and to you, the purchaser of these books! You are helping some wonderful teachers continue their programs in your schools!

Thanks to All of You,

Grady W. Reed

Grady W. Reed, Owner, California Cookbook Company

P.S. Please note the RE-ORDER FORM on page 159.

Table of Contents

On our Front Cover, and page 51:
Fire Roasted Tomato and Garlic Pizza
Courtesy of Borden Foods, Columbus, Ohio

Simone Clements
Bret Harte High School, Angels Camp

Carol Delap
Golden West High School, Visalia

Cindy Elledge
Johansen High School, Modesto

Pam Fecchino
Cimarron-Memorial High School,
Las Vegas, NV

Pam Ford
Temecula Valley High School,
Temecula

Debbie Harvey
Amador Valley High School,
Pleasanton

Carol Goddard
Alhambra High School, Alhambra

Donna Hamilton
Del Oro High School, Loomis

Gerry Henderson
Temple City High School, Temple City

Gage Hewes
So. Pasadena High School,
So. Pasadena

Grace Hibma
Office of L.A. County Superintendent
of Schools, Consultant Consumer &
Homemaking Education

Donna Hulen
Career Consultant Los Alamitos High
School, Los Alamitos

Dotti Jones
Etiwanda High School, Etiwanda

Mary Lash
Paramount High School, Paramount

Helen Lievre
La Cañada High School, La Cañada

Karen Lopez
San Luis Obispo High School,
San Luis Obispo

Jeri Lundy
Grossmont High School, La Mesa

Darlene Lupul
Tokay High School, Lodi

Dale Matsuno
Bell Gardens High School,
Bell Gardens

Doris Oitzman
Victor Valley High School, Victorville

Linda Paskins
Cordova High School,
Rancho Cordova

Mary Rector
Valley High School, Las Vegas, NV

Betty Rabin
Sierra Vista Jr. High School,
Canyon Country

April Rosendahl
Chino High School, Chino

Lynda Ruth
La Mirada High School, La Mirada

Marianne Traw
Ball Junior High School, Anaheim

Sonja Tyree
Ayala High School, Chino Hills

Sue Walters
Morse High School, San Diego

Betty Wells
Bidwell Junior High School, Chico

Kathryn P. Whitten
Regional Supervisor
Home Economics Education, Fresno

Appetizers

ARTICHOKE FRITTATA

Serves 6 - 8

- 1 (13.75 ounce) can water packed artichoke hearts
- 1 (14 ounce) can mushrooms, stems and pieces
- 1/3 cup yellow onion, chopped
- 2 (large) cloves garlic, crushed
- 1 rib celery, chopped
- 5 large eggs
- 4 sprigs parsley, chopped
- 2 tablespoons olive oil
- 1/3 cup Parmesan cheese, shredded
- 1/4 cup cheddar cheese, shredded
- dash Tabasco sauce
- salt and pepper, to taste
- nonstick cooking spray

Rinse, drain and chop artichokes. Drain mushrooms. Heat skillet to high heat. Add artichokes, mushrooms, onion, garlic and celery; heat 3 to 4 minutes, covered. Remove from heat. In a large bowl, slightly beat eggs with remaining ingredients, fold in heated vegetables. Spray an ovenproof frying pan with nonstick cooking spray. Pour mixture into pan and cook until mixture forms an outer crust, 3 to 4 minutes. Place in oven and bake 20 to 25 minutes, until set. Cool, cut, and turn out on plate.

"This recipe came to me from Agnes Gogna, a neighbor of over 60 years."

Darlene Lupul   **Tokay High School, Lodi, CA**

Pasta should be cooked al dente, which means "to the tooth". Pasta should be chewy, but not crunchy or even soft. Pasta continues to cook even after it is drained. By tasting with your tooth, look for a pinhole and drain immediately.

Donna Leslie   **Menlo-Atherton HS, Menlo Park, CA**

BASIL & SUN-DRIED TOMATO CHEESE TORTA

Serves 24

Cream Cheese Mixture:
3 pounds cream cheese, softened
$\frac{1}{4}$ pound unsalted butter, softened
$\frac{1}{2}$ cup Parmesan cheese, freshly grated
1 tablespoons dried thyme
1 tablespoons minced garlic
1 teaspoon salt
$\frac{1}{2}$ teaspoon ground white pepper

Basil Pesto:
3 cups fresh basil leaves
6 cloves garlic, minced
$\frac{1}{2}$ cup pine nuts
$\frac{1}{4}$ cup extra-virgin olive oil
1 teaspoon fresh lemon juice
$\frac{1}{2}$ teaspoon salt
$\frac{1}{2}$ teaspoon freshly ground black pepper
$\frac{1}{4}$ cup Parmesan cheese, freshly grated

Sun-Dried Tomato Pesto:
1 $\frac{1}{2}$ cups sun-dried tomatoes, soaked in
    2 cups hot water 30 minutes, or until softened
$\frac{1}{2}$ cup pine nuts
8 cloves garlic, minced
$\frac{1}{4}$ cup extra-virgin olive oil
$\frac{1}{2}$ teaspoon salt
$\frac{1}{2}$ teaspoon black pepper, freshly ground
$\frac{1}{4}$ cup Parmesan cheese, freshly grated

Cream Cheese Mixture: In bowl of a food processor fitted with metal blade, combine cream cheese and butter; process until smooth, about 30 seconds. Add Parmesan, thyme, garlic, salt and pepper; process a few seconds more. Transfer to a bowl and set aside.

Basil Pesto: In bowl of a food processor fitted with metal blade, combine basil, garlic, pine nuts, olive oil, lemon juice, salt and pepper; process until smooth, about 2 minutes. Add Parmesan and process a few seconds more. Transfer mixture to a bowl and set aside.

Sun-Dried Tomato Pesto: Remove softened tomatoes from water and squeeze out liquid. In bowl of a food processor fitted with metal blade, combine tomatoes with pine nuts, garlic, olive oil, salt and pepper; process until smooth, about 2 minutes. Add Parmesan and process a few seconds more. Transfer mixture to bowl, set aside.

To Assemble Torte: Line inside of a 2 quart glass or metal bowl with plastic wrap. Put a 2 $\frac{1}{2}$" thick layer of Cream Cheese Mixture on bottom of bowl. Add a $\frac{1}{2}$" thick layer of Sun Dried Tomato Pesto, extending evenly to the sides of the mold. Add a $\frac{1}{2}$" thick layer of Basil Pesto, extending it evenly to the sides of the mold. Repeat until you reach the top of the mold, ending with a layer of cream cheese. Fold ends of plastic wrap over top of mold to cover and press down with your hands to compress mold. Refrigerate at least 6 hours, or until torta is firm. Unmold onto a serving platter and surround with Garlic Toasts or your favorite crackers. NOTE: This can be made up to 2 days in advance.

Betty Rabin   **Sierra Vista Junior High School, Canyon Country, CA**

BRUSCHETTA BY JANE

Serves 6

- 2 large cloves garlic, minced
- ½ cup olive oil
- 1 baguette bread
- 4 Roma tomatoes, chopped
- ¼ cup fresh basil, chopped
- ¼ cup Parmesan cheese, freshly grated

Preheat oven to 350 degrees. Mix garlic and olive oil together in a small bowl. Slice baguette into ½" thick slices. Brush bread slices with some of the olive oil mixture and place on a cookie sheet. Bake 10 minutes, turning over halfway through baking. Add chopped tomatoes and basil to remaining garlic/olive oil and spoon onto toasted bread slices. Sprinkle with cheese and serve.

"This is a beautiful Italian appetizer, and it's nutritious too.
Low in saturated fat, high in veggies."

Jane Souza   **No. Monterey Co. High School, Castroville, CA**

CAPPUCCINO

- 2 ounces instant coffee
- 1 pound coffee creamer
- 1 ½ pounds sweetened cocoa mix
- 2 teaspoons ground cinnamon
- 1 teaspoon ground nutmeg
- *Garnish:* Whipped Cream

For Large Quantities:

- 4 ounces instant coffee (⅓ of a 12 ounce jar)
- 1 (35.3 ounce) jar coffee creamer
- 1 (3 pound, 2 ounce) can sweetened cocoa mix
- 4 teaspoons ground cinnamon
- 2 teaspoons ground nutmeg
- *Garnish:* Whipped Cream

Mix all ingredients and store in airtight container. To serve, put 3 rounded teaspoons in a mug of hot water. Stir well. Top with whipped cream. NOTE: Use a heaping ⅓ cup measure for a large 12 ounce mug.

"We have used this recipe for fundraising at Back To School Nights or football games, etc."

Peg Ellington   **Yucca Valley High School, Yucca Valley, CA**

CROSTINIS

Serves 4 - 6

- 1 cup cheddar cheese, grated
- ½ cup mozzarella cheese, grated
- 1 can tomato sauce
- 1 can olives, chopped
- 4 green onions, chopped
- 2 cloves garlic, chopped
- ⅓ cup oil
- English muffins or French bread, sliced in half

Mix all ingredients, except bread, together in a bowl. Spread on English muffin halves or sliced French bread and bake at 300 degrees for 15 minutes. NOTE: Can be

7

kept in refrigerator up to a week.

"A student of mine shared this family favorite in a class demonstration several years ago."
Cheryle Apple   **Rio Vista High School, Rio Vista, CA**

FOCACCIA BREAD
Makes 24

   1 package dry yeast
   1 cup warm water
   2 teaspoons sugar
   $\frac{3}{4}$ teaspoon salt
   $\frac{1}{4}$ cup vegetable oil
   2 $\frac{2}{3}$ to 3 cups all-purpose flour
   olive oil
   $\frac{1}{2}$ cup fresh basil, thinly sliced
   1 cup fontina or Gorgonzola cheese (or mixture of both)

In a large bowl, sprinkle yeast over warm water and let stand 5 minutes. Stir in sugar, salt and vegetable oil. Add 2 cups flour, mixing to blend. Beat an additional 2 to 4 minutes. Stir in about $\frac{2}{3}$ cup more flour to make a soft dough. Turn dough out on lightly floured surface. Knead until smooth, about 8 minutes. Place in greased bowl to let rise 1 hour or can be refrigerated overnight. Roll dough to 10" x 15" rectangle. Place in greased sheet pan. Brush surface with olive oil, sprinkle with basil and cheese. Let rise $\frac{1}{2}$ hour. Bake at 450 degrees 12 to 15 minutes.

Betty Wells   **Bidwell Junior High School, Chico, CA**

FRESH GARLIC BREAD WITH A TWIST
Makes 1 loaf

   1 loaf French bread
   $\frac{1}{4}$ cup olive oil
   2 to 3 cloves garlic
   $\frac{1}{4}$ cup Parmesan cheese, grated
   1 $\frac{1}{2}$ teaspoons dried basil
   1 teaspoon dried oregano

Slice French bread into $\frac{3}{4}$" slices; set aside. Heat oil in frying pan and saute garlic until golden brown. Dip each piece of bread in oil, flat side down, to absorb oil and garlic. Sprinkle each slice with Parmesan, basil and oregano. Broil until golden brown. Serve immediately.

"A healthy alternative to garlic bread but much tastier than the traditional."
Laury White   **Fallbrook High School, Fallbrook, CA**

FRIED ARTICHOKE HEARTS
Makes 20

   1 pound cocktail artichokes. fresh or frozen
   $\frac{1}{2}$ cup flour
   $\frac{1}{2}$ teaspoon salt
   1 egg, well beaten
   1 cup milk
   1 teaspoon baking powder
   oil, for frying
   Garnish: vinegar, salt and pepper

Trim all tough outer leaves off artichokes. Cut off thorns and trim bottom from remaining heart. Slice artichokes lengthwise into thirds. Prepare batter by combining flour, salt, egg, milk and baking powder. Heat oil to 370 degrees. Dip artichokes in batter and fry in oil until golden brown. Serve with splashes of vinegar and a little salt and pepper. Drain on paper towels.

Kris Mehan   Oroville` High School, Oroville, CA

FRIED MOZZARELLA CHEESE STICKS
Serves 4 - 8

1 pound mozzarella cheese
½ cup flour
1 cup bread crumbs
½ teaspoon garlic powder
½ teaspoon oregano
½ teaspoon ground cumin
pinch salt and pepper
3 large eggs
½ to 1 cup vegetable oil, for frying
1 cup marinara sauce

Cut mozzarella into sticks about ¼" x 1 ½" long. Coat sticks with flour; shaking off excess. Combine bread crumbs and seasonings in a flat dish. Beat eggs in small bowl. Coat sticks by dipping in egg, then bread crumb mixture. (You may repeat if you prefer heavy coating.) Heat 2" oil in fry pan over medium-high heat. Deep fry sticks 3 to 4 minutes, until golden brown. Keep warm in oven until all sticks are fried. Serve with marinara sauce for dipping.

Libby Newman   West Valley High School, Hemet, CA

GARLIC PARMESAN PULL-APARTS
Serves 16

nonstick cooking spray
⅓ cup margarine, melted
1 cup Parmesan cheese, grated
1 teaspoon black pepper
2 cloves garlic, pressed
2 packages refrigerator dinner rolls

Preheat oven to 375 degrees. Use cooking spray to coat the bottom and sides of a fluted bundt pan. Melt butter and set aside. Combine Parmesan cheese, black pepper and garlic in mixing bowl. Separate dinner rolls and cut into fourths. Dip in melted butter, then in cheese mixture. Arrange evenly through pan. Bake 30 minutes.

"Easy fun and looks beautiful."

Tracie Priske   Valencia High School, Valencia, CA

When baking cooked pasta, slightly undercook the pasta, otherwise it will turn to mush after being baked.

Diane Lizardi   Downey HS, Downey, CA

Hot Anchovy Dip (Bagna Caoda)
Serves 4

3 Italian sausages
$\frac{1}{2}$ cup butter
1 $\frac{1}{4}$ cups olive oil
12 cloves garlic, peeled
1 can anchovy fillets, drained
1 cup half & half
1 head curly cabbage, washed, chilled
4 stalks celery, cut into serving sized pieces, chilled
1 jar marinated roasted red peppers, drained
1 loaf French bread

Cook sausages by boiling them in water for about 25 minutes. Cut into $\frac{1}{4}$" slices and set aside. Melt butter and mix with olive oil in a small electric skillet. When butter foams, add garlic. Continue cooking on low until garlic becomes soft. Mash garlic and add anchovy fillets. Cook until well blended. Add half & half right before serving, adding more half & half if it becomes too thick. Arrange cabbage on platter with celery, sausages and roasted peppers. Dip vegetables and sausages into hot garlic mixture long enough to heat. Serve with a fresh loaf of French bread.

"I make this Italian fondue on New Year's Eve! Most can't believe there are anchovies."
Linda Brayton   **Grace Davis High School, Modesto, CA**

Italian Butter
Makes $\frac{1}{2}$ cup

$\frac{1}{2}$ cup butter, at room temperature
2 teaspoons lemon juice
1 tablespoon basil
$\frac{1}{2}$ teaspoon oregano
$\frac{1}{2}$ teaspoon garlic salt

Combine butter and seasonings; beat until light and fluffy.

"This quick spread is especially good on zucchini, green beans, chicken, veal and bread."
Amber Bradley   **Granite Hills High School, El Cajon, CA**

Marinated Broccoli
Serves 4

1 $\frac{1}{2}$ pounds broccoli florets
1 cup olive oil
2 lemons, juiced
salt and pepper, to taste
8 cloves garlic, sliced

Blanch broccoli and chill at least 6 hours. Place broccoli in large bowl. Add olive oil, lemon juice, salt and pepper to taste. Add garlic and toss. Chill 8 hours or overnight.

"This is a favorite appetizer from Giorgio's Italian Restaurant in Hesperia."
Nancy Earnest   **Victor Valley High School, Victorville, CA**

MINI CALZONE
Makes 16

1 loaf frozen bread dough, thawed
9 slices hard salami, chopped
5 to 6 mushrooms, chopped
$\frac{1}{4}$ cup onion, chopped
$\frac{1}{3}$ cup spaghetti sauce
$\frac{1}{2}$ cup mozzarella cheese, shredded
1 tablespoon yellow cornmeal

Divide loaf of dough into 16 pieces. In a medium bowl, combine all remaining ingredients except cornmeal; mix well. Set aside. Sprinkle cutting board with flour. Flatten each piece of dough on the board into a circle 2 to 3" in diameter. Fill with 2 tablespoons filling. Fold dough over and seal edges. Place on a greased cookie sheet which has been dusted with cornmeal. Place calzones 1 to 2" apart. Bake at 375 degrees 10 to 12 minutes.

Diane Castro   **Temecula Valley High School, Temecula, CA**

MOZZARELLA & PESTO CRESCENT TARTS
Serves 16

1 (8 ounce) can Pillsbury Refrigerated Crescent Dinner Rolls
2 tablespoons pesto
2 (medium) tomatoes, seeded, sliced
1 (small) red onion, thinly sliced
1 teaspoon fresh rosemary, chopped or
    $\frac{1}{2}$ teaspoon dried rosemary leaves
$\frac{1}{2}$ cup fresh mozzarella cheese, diced or shredded
$\frac{1}{4}$ cup Parmesan cheese, freshly shredded

Heat oven to 425 degrees. Unroll dough into 2 long rectangles. Place 3" apart on ungreased cookie sheet. Firmly press perforations to seal. Press to form two 10" x 3" strips, forming rim around edge of dough. Spread each strip with 1 tablespoon pesto. Top each with tomatoes, onion and rosemary. Sprinkle each with mozzarella and Parmesan cheeses. Bake 10 to 14 minutes, or until edges are golden brown and cheese is melted. Cut each into crosswise slices. Serve warm or cool.

"This was a student demo, completed by Adam Edwards and Megan Nelson, for my Foods 2 class."

Debbie Harvey   **Amador Valley High School, Pleasanton, CA**

Capicola is a spicy, tender Italian ham that is similar to prosciutto.

Jan Schulenburg   **Irvine HS, Irvine, CA**

OLIVE SPREAD

Makes 12

- 1 can black olives, chopped
- 1 can Ortega chiles, chopped
- 6 green onions, minced
- 1 clove garlic minced
- 1 $\frac{1}{2}$ cups sharp cheddar cheese
- $\frac{1}{3}$ cup olive oil
- 1 small can tomato sauce
- 1 teaspoon Italian seasoning
- 1 teaspoon oregano
- 1 teaspoon garlic salt
- 1 loaf French bread, sliced horizontally or
    - 1 package sourdough English muffins

Combine all ingredients, except bread. Spread on French bread or English muffins. Put under broiler until bubbly. Serve immediately. NOTE: You may add salami, cheese, pepper, onions, etc. for topping.

Donna Fippin   **Bret Harte High School, Altaville, CA**

ORANGE/LEMON APPETIZERS

Serves 4

- 6 seedless Sunkist oranges
- 6 lemons
- 1 cup olive oil
- salt and pepper

Peel and slice oranges and lemons $\frac{1}{8}$" thick. Put in bowl with olive oil. Salt and pepper, to taste. Chill 6 hours. To serve, lay slices in a circle alternately on a plate.

"This recipe is from Giorgio's Italian Restaurant in Hesperia.
It has been in the owner, Joseph Guarini's family for over 60 years."

Nancy Earnest   **Victor Valley High School, Victorville, CA**

PARMESAN PULL APARTS

Serves 8

- $\frac{1}{4}$ cup margarine
- 1 teaspoon celery flakes
- $\frac{1}{2}$ teaspoon onion flakes
- 1 teaspoon parsley flakes
- 1 package refrigerator biscuits
- 1 to 2 tablespoons Parmesan cheese, grated

Melt margarine in round cake pan in oven as oven is preheating to 425 degrees. When melted, remove from oven and crumble celery, onion and parsley flakes over melted margarine. Cut each biscuit into quarters and place on margarine-herb mixture in pan. Sprinkle with Parmesan cheese. Bake 12 to 15 minutes or until golden brown. Let set 1 minute, then invert on plate. Serve hot.

"I got this recipe when I was in junior high school many years ago."

Shirley Marshman   **West Middle School, Downey, CA**

PEPPERONI PIZZA DIP

Makes 1 1/2 cups

1 (8 ounce) package cream cheese, softened
1/2 cup dairy sour cream
1 teaspoon dried oregano, crushed
1/8 teaspoon garlic powder
1/2 cup pizza sauce
1/2 cup pepperoni, chopped
1/4 cup green onion, sliced
1/4 cup green pepper, chopped
1/2 cup mozzarella cheese, shredded
Raw vegetables, chips, crackers or crusty bread

In small mixer bowl, beat together cream cheese, sour cream, oregano and garlic powder. Spread evenly in a 9" or 10" quiche dish or pie plate. Spread pizza sauce over the top. Sprinkle with pepperoni, green onion and green pepper. Bake at 350 degrees for 10 minutes. Top with cheese; bake 5 minutes more, until cheese is melted and mixture is heated through. Serve with raw vegetables, chips, crackers or crusty bread.

Carol Goddard   **Alhambra High School, Alhambra, CA**

PIZZA BITES

Makes 20

2 packages refrigerated biscuits
1/2 cup pizza sauce
1/2 cup mozzarella cheese, grated
1/3 cup pepperoni
Garnish: Parmesan cheese, grated

Preheat oven to 350 degrees. Flatten biscuits into 3" circles. Combine sauce, cheese and pepperoni in a small bowl. Place a large teaspoonful of pizza mixture on top of each flattened biscuit. Gather edges together to make a bundle and seal well. Place on foil-lined baking sheet, seam side down. Sprinkle with Parmesan cheese. Bake 12 to 15 minutes, or until light brown. Serve hot.

Betty Getchell   **La Mirada High School, La Mirada, CA**

PIZZA POCKETS

Makes 36

Dough:
2 packages dry yeast
$\frac{1}{2}$ teaspoon sugar
1 $\frac{1}{4}$ cups warm water (105 to 115 degrees)
3 $\frac{1}{2}$ cups unsifted flour
1 teaspoon salt
$\frac{1}{4}$ cup oil
Filling:
$\frac{1}{2}$ pound mushrooms, sliced
3 tablespoons onion, chopped
1 clove garlic, crushed
3 tablespoons oil
8 ounces tomato sauce
$\frac{1}{3}$ pound salami, sliced
salt and pepper, to taste
2 $\frac{1}{4}$ ounces olives, sliced
1 teaspoons dried oregano
1 teaspoon dried basil
$\frac{1}{2}$ teaspoon sugar
$\frac{1}{4}$ teaspoon crushed red pepper
salt and pepper, to taste
2 $\frac{1}{3}$ cups mozzarella cheese, shredded
1 tablespoon cornmeal

Dough: Sprinkle yeast and sugar over $\frac{1}{4}$ cup warm water. Let stand 2 to 3 minutes without stirring. Then stir until yeast and sugar are completely dissolved. Set in prewarmed oven 3 to 5 minutes. Stir flour and salt together in large bowl. Make a well and pour in yeast mixture, 1 cup warm water and oil. Mix all together into ball. Place on floured surface and knead 15 minutes, or use mixer with dough hook 10 minutes. Place in oiled bowl, turning dough once to coat. Cover with oiled waxed paper and damp towel. Let dough rise about 45 minutes, until doubled in size. After dough has risen, punch down, divide into four parts. Roll dough to no more than $\frac{1}{8}$" thick. Cut into 9" rounds for appetizers or 11" to 12" rounds for dinner.

Filling: Saute vegetables in oil until limp; drain excess oil. Add tomato sauce, salami, olives, oregano, basil, sugar and red pepper. Salt and pepper, to taste. Simmer 5 minutes. Cool. Stir in shredded cheese.

Divide up filling and place on half round . Fold edge up and over. Seal and crimp. Repeat until all dough and filling is used. Place on greased baking sheet that has been dusted with cornmeal. Poke holes in tops with fork and brush with oil. Bake at 475 degrees about 10 minutes, until browned.

"These are a definite favorite of students; work, but well worth it."

Simone Clements   **Bret Harte High School, Angel Camp, CA**

Pizza Swirls
Serves 6

1 (10 ounce) can refrigerated pizza crust or
    1 recipe of short cut pizza dough
2 tablespoons pesto sauce
$\frac{1}{2}$ cup pizza sauce
$\frac{1}{2}$ cup pepperoni, sliced
$\frac{1}{4}$ cup black olives, chopped
1 cup Italian blend cheeses, shredded (or your favorite cheese)

Heat oven to 400 degrees. Grease a cookie sheet. Unroll dough and press into a 10" x 12" rectangle. Spread pesto sauce to within $\frac{1}{2}$" of edge. Combine pizza sauce, pepperoni and olives. Spread over pesto sauce. Sprinkle on cheese and press lightly. Starting at the long side, roll up dough tightly, in jelly roll fashion. Cut the roll across into 1" slices. Arrange slices on cookie sheet and bake 10 to 12 minutes or until light golden in color. Let stand 5 minutes. Serve warm or at room temperature.

"Make packets by cutting the dough into 3 squares, filling with pesto, pizza sauce and cheese, and bringing corners to the center and pinching together tightly.

Roberta Marshall   **Deer Valley High School, Antioch, CA**

Ricotta Puffs
Serves 9

1 sheet frozen puff pastry, thawed
$\frac{1}{2}$ cup ricotta cheese
$\frac{1}{2}$ cup red pepper, chopped
3 tablespoons Romano cheese, grated
1 tablespoon parsley, snipped
1 teaspoon oregano
$\frac{1}{2}$ teaspoon pepper
$\frac{1}{2}$ cup milk
Garnish: grated Romano cheese

Preheat oven to 400 degrees. Cut pastry into nine 3" squares. For filling, mix remaining ingredients together, except milk and cheese for garnish. Moisten edges of pastry squares with milk. Spoon 2 teaspoons filling onto 1 side of square. Fold the other side over filling and seal. Cut slits into top of pastry. Brush with milk; sprinkle with Romano cheese. Bake 20 minutes.

Deanna Olsen   **Cerro Villa Middle School, Villa Park, CA**

Roasted Garlic with Gorgonzola
Serves 4

Garlic oil:
1 (large) head garlic
$\frac{1}{2}$ cup extra virgin olive oil
Cream Sauce:
1 cup heavy cream
1 cup Gorgonzola cheese, crumbled (about 4.5 ounces)
1 baguette or loaf French bread

Garlic oil: Preheat oven to 450 degrees. Wrap garlic in foil and roast in middle of oven until tender, about 45 minutes. Carefully unwrap and cool. Halve the garlic head and separate into cloves. Peel cloves. In small bowl, add oil to garlic and let stand covered, chilled for 2 to 3 days.

Cream Sauce: Boil cream, stirring occasionally, until reduced to about $\frac{1}{2}$ cup. Add Gorgonzola and cook over low heat, stirring constantly, until cheese melts and sauce is smooth. Remove pan from heat and keep sauce warm, covered. Cut bread in half; brush with garlic oil. Broil 2 to 3 inches from heat until golden. Cut into 1" slices. Put warm cheese in middle of plate. Arrange bread on sides. Dip bread in sauce.

"I got this from Bon Appetit's website."

Penny Childers   **Ramona High School, Ramona, CA**

STUFFED MUSHROOMS
Serves 15

    12 ounces Italian sausage
    8 ounces cream cheese
    1 $\frac{1}{2}$ teaspoons Worcestershire sauce
    25 to 30 fresh mushrooms

Brown sausage; drain grease. Combine with cream cheese and Worcestershire sauce; mash together. Wash mushrooms; remove stems. Fill each mushroom cap with sausage filling. Place on baking sheet and broil until browned and hot.

"A favorite of our customers at the Legacy Restaurant, in Jordan High School."

Marci D. Morgan   **Jordan High School, Salt Lake City, UT**

SUMMER SAUSAGE
Makes 5 loaves

    5 pounds (30% fat) hamburger
    4 tablespoons Morton Quik Curing Salt
    2 $\frac{1}{2}$ teaspoons liquid smoke
    3 teaspoons mustard seeds
    3 teaspoons coarse ground pepper
    1 $\frac{1}{2}$ teaspoons garlic powder

Mix all ingredients together. Shape in to 5 round 12" loaves. Cover and place in refrigerator overnight. Bake on a broiler pan, uncovered, 9 hours at 150 degrees. Turn loaves over half way through cooking.

"My cousin shared this recipe with me while we were touring the west coast of Oregon. It's excellent sliced thin and served with cheese and crackers!"

Jill Sweet-Gregory   **Santa Paula High School, Santa Paula, CA**

TAMPENADE (OLIVE PATÉ)
Makes 3 cups

    2 cups canned green olives, pitted, no pimiento
    1 cup whole black olives, pitted
    5 - 6 cloves garlic, crushed
    3 tablespoons olive oil
    thin slices Italian bread or crackers, for serving
    Garnish: Bright colored, thinly sliced vegetables,
        such as radishes or red bell pepper

Place all ingredients, except garnish, in blender. Blend until all pieces of olive are small, forming a spread. (Add more olive oil, a few drops at at time, if not spreading consistency.) Store in refrigerator until serving time. Serve with thin slices of Italian bread or crackers. Garnish with desired vegetables. NOTE: You might want to use less garlic or more, to your taste. Start with 5 cloves, and add the 6th, if desired.

"If you like olives, you'll be crazy about this spread!"

Judy Henry   **Newhart Middle School, Mission Viejo, CA**

VEGETABLE MARINADE

2 cups carrots, sliced
2 cups onions, sliced
2 cups celery, cut into 1-inch lengths
2 cups peppers, cut in chunks
2 cups green olives
2 cups pepperoncini peppers
Marinade:
1 cup red wine vinegar
1 cup white wine vinegar
½ teaspoon salt
1 teaspoon oregano
1 teaspoon coarse black pepper

In a large crock pot, place vegetables. Cover with marinade and refrigerate 12 hours. Serve.

"This is a wonderful vegetable marinade. This recipe is from the Della Fontana restaurant."

Kathy Rudelich   **Hillcrest High School, Midvale, UT**

Cook plenty of pasta; refrigerate in ziploc bags. When needed, simply take pasta out, dip in boiling water, and it's ready to eat! Spices should be added during the last 10 minutes of cooking time for more flavor. Dried spices give more flavor than ground spices. Paprika is a wonderful tasty substitute for chili powder. Paprika will give you a cheese flavor when used in sauces, especially white sauces.

Catherine Diaz   **Exeter HS, Exeter, CA**

These can be entire meals!
Soups & Salads

ANTIPASTO SALAD
Serves 6

6 cups assorted salad greens
4 eggs, hard cooked, peeled, sliced
½ red onion, thinly sliced
1 red pepper, sliced
1 green pepper, sliced
1 jar marinated artichoke hearts, drained
6 fresh mushrooms, sliced
2 (small) zucchini sliced
1 can anchovy fillets, drained
1 (small) can olives, sliced
1 (large) tomato, cut into wedges
Prepared Oil & Vinegar dressing

Wash and thoroughly dry salad greens. Arrange in a large flat bowl or basket. Top with remaining ingredients, arranging in an artistic manner. Pour salad dressing over all. NOTE: For increased flavor, onion, peppers, mushroom and zucchini may be marinated in oil-vinegar dressing several hours before salad is assembled.

Ramona Anderson   **Mira Mesa High School, San Diego, CA**

ARTICHOKE PASTA SALAD
Serves 4 - 6

½ pound corkscrew pasta, cooked, drained
¼ cup Parmesan cheese, grated
½ cup Italian bread crumbs
½ cup celery, chopped
⅓ cup green pepper, chopped
1 medium tomato, diced
¼ cup red onion, chopped
1 can black olives, drained
1 can garbanzo beans
Good Seasons Italian Dressing Mix
2 jars marinated artichoke hearts, undrained
salt and pepper, to taste

In a large bowl, combine all ingredients; toss gently. Season with salt and pepper, to taste. Serve chilled.

"This pasta salad is very colorful with an excellent blend of flavors."

Laura Tittle   **Pleasant Valley High School, Chico, CA**

CHICKEN PASTA SALAD
Serves 8

2 cups chicken, cooked, diced
1 cup red pepper, cubed
2 cups mozzarella cheese, grated
1 (large) red onion, sliced
1 pound red pepper pasta, cooked, cooled
2 cups bottled Italian dressing
Garnish: Diced avocado, crushed taco chips

In large bowl, toss together chicken, red pepper, cheese, onion and pasta. Add salad dressing, making sure pasta absorbs the dressing. Arrange avocado and crushed taco chips over top.

Myrna Westmoreland   **Grace Davis High School, Modesto, CA**

CHICKEN PASTA SOUP
Serves 6 - 8

3 tablespoons butter
4 ounces button mushrooms, sliced
1 cup celery, sliced
1 cup carrots, shredded
1 (medium) onion, chopped
3 tablespoons flour
6 cups chicken stock
1 $\frac{1}{2}$ cups half & half
2 tablespoons parsley, chopped
3 boneless, skinless chicken breast halves, cut into half-inch pieces
1 cup penne pasta
$\frac{1}{4}$ cup sugar snap peas, halved diagonally
3 tablespoons lemon juice
salt and pepper, to taste

In large pot, melt butter. Add mushrooms, celery, carrots and onion; cook until tender, about 5 minutes. Stir in flour and cook 3 minutes, stirring frequently. Gradually stir in chicken stock; bring to a simmer, stirring frequently. Add half & half and parsley; simmer 5 minutes. Add chicken and simmer until chicken is cooked through, about 5 minutes. (At this point, soup can be refrigerated and finished later or the next day.) Cook penne pasta until tender but firm to bite; drain. Bring chicken soup to a simmer. Mix in cooked pasta, sugar snap peas and simmer 2 minutes. Stir in lemon juice and season with salt and pepper, to taste.

"You can replace chicken with scallops or shrimp. This is a good, creamy soup."

Penny Childers   **Ramona High School, Ramona, CA**

19

CHICKEN PESTO PASTA SALAD
Serves 6

3 chicken breasts, grilled or baked
1 pound penne pasta, cooked, drained
1 ½ cups pesto (Trader Joe's)
⅔ jar sun-dried tomatoes in oil, chopped
4 ounces feta cheese, crumbled
¾ cup artichoke hearts (optional)
¾ cup Kalamata olives, halved
Garnish: Parmesan cheese, freshly grated (optional)

Cut cooked chicken into bite-sized pieces. Combine pasta with pesto, sun-dried tomatoes, feta cheese and artichokes (if using); mix well. Add chicken and olives, stir to mix. Serve with freshly grated Parmesan cheese.

"Great for a quick, family dinner."

Beverly Ranger　　　　　**Carpinteria Junior High School, Carpinteria, CA**

CHRISTMAS PASTA SALAD
Serves 10

1 package specialty pasta
1 bunch spinach
2 tomatoes, diced
8 mushrooms, sliced
1 bunch (or less) green onions, chopped
1 bottle Caesar salad dressing
¼ cup pine nuts
⅓ cup Parmesan cheese, freshly grated

Cook pasta al dente; drain and cool. Wash and tear spinach leaves and place in a large bowl. Toss with cooked pasta, tomatoes, mushrooms and green onions. Just before serving toss with salad dressing and pine nuts (as they will get soggy if added too soon). Sprinkle with Parmesan cheese and serve.

"I found this salad at the country club for their Christmas buffet."

Carole Call　　　　　**Costa Mesa High School, Costa Mesa, CA**

I add about 1 tablespoon olive oil to the boiling water to keep noodles or pasta from sticking. I like the pasta al dente, or firm to the bite, so I cut it with a spoon against the pot and if it cuts cleanly, it's done.

Faye Nielsen　　　　　**Rosemead HS, Rosemead, CA**

CIOPPINO

Serves 6

- 1 (28 ounce) can tomatoes, undrained, cut up
- 1 (16 ounce) can stewed tomatoes, undrained, cut up
- 1 (8 ounce) can tomato sauce
- 1 cup dry white wine
- 2 teaspoons basil leaves
- 1 teaspoon salt
- $\frac{1}{4}$ teaspoon pepper
- 12 small clams, in shell, washed
- $\frac{1}{3}$ cup olive oil
- 1 $\frac{1}{2}$ cups onion, chopped
- 1 cup fresh parsley, chopped
- 1 pound fresh (medium) shrimp, shelled, deveined
- 6 cloves garlic, minced
- 1 pound frozen snow or dungeness crab legs
- 1 pound fresh halibut or cod, cut into 1 $\frac{1}{2}$" pieces
- French bread

In 5 quart Dutch oven, combine tomatoes, stewed tomatoes, tomato sauce, wine, basil, salt and pepper. Bring to a boil. Reduce heat and simmer, uncovered, 10 minutes, stirring occasionally. Bring back to a boil. Add clams. Cover tightly and cook over medium heat 4 to 6 minutes, or until clam shells open. In medium saucepan, heat oil. Stir in onions, parsley, shrimp and garlic. Simmer, covered, 3 to 5 minutes or until shrimp are light pink, stirring occasionally. Stir shrimp mixture into tomato-clam mixture. Add crab. Simmer, uncovered 5 minutes. Add fish pieces. Simmer, uncovered, an additional 2 to 3 minutes or until fish flakes easily with fork. Serve with thick slices of French bread to dip in rich broth.

"We traditionally make on New Year's Day. A lot of the preparation can be done ahead of time, such as the chopping of garlic, onion, parsley and the cleaning of the fish."

Sheila Ryan Kerber　　　　　**Actis Junior High School, Bakersfield, CA**

EASY MINESTRONE

Serves 4

1 ½ cups water
1 ½ cups beef broth
2 tablespoons barley
1 ½ cups stewed tomatoes, with their juice
½ cup carrots, diced
¼ cup elbow macaroni
1 tablespoon oil
½ cup onion, diced
½ cup celery, diced
1 clove garlic, minced
½ pound stew meat, diced
¼ teaspoon oregano, crumbled
¼ teaspoon thyme
¼ teaspoon basil
7 ounces kidney beans
½ cup cooked corn
½ cup cooked green beans
salt and pepper, to taste
Garnish: Parmesan cheese, grated

Combine water and broth in a large pot; bring to a boil. Add barley and simmer, covered, 20 minutes. Add tomatoes, carrots and macaroni. Cover and continue to simmer. Meanwhile, heat oil in frying pan. Saute onion and celery for 4 to 5 minutes; add garlic, meat, oregano, thyme and basil. Cook until meat browns. Add meat mixture to soup, along with kidney beans, corn and green beans. Season with salt and pepper. Serve with Parmesan cheese.

Faith Gobuty   **Woodside High School, Woodside, CA**

EASY PASTA SALAD

Serves 6 - 8

16 ounces spiral pasta
8 ounces mozzarella cheese, cut into bite-sized cubes
1 red bell pepper, cut into bite-sized pieces
1 bottle Bernstein's Cheese Fantastic Italian Dressing
1 (16 ounce) package frozen peas

Cook pasta according to package directions until al dente; drain and cool. Combine all ingredients and chill well. Serve cold.

"Other vegetables can be added. The amount of Italian dressing can be adjusted according to individual tastes. Easy and quick. This salad always receives lots of compliments."

April Rosendahl   **Chino High School, Chino, CA**

FAVORITE MINESTRONE SOUP

Serves 8

2 tablespoons olive oil
1 (large) onion, chopped
2 cloves garlic, peeled, minced
2 stalks celery, chopped
1 tablespoons parsley, chopped
1 tablespoon basil leaves
1 teaspoon sugar
1 quart beef stock
1 ½ quarts water
2 (15 ounce) cans kidney beans, drained
2 zucchini, sliced
1 cup tomato sauce
1 teaspoon oregano leaves
2 (15 ounce) cans garbanzo beans (chick peas), drained
1 (large) potato, peeled, cubed
1 cup cabbage, chopped
1 cup fresh green beans, cut into 1-inch pieces
1 cup macaroni

Garnish: Parmesan cheese, freshly grated. Salt and pepper to taste.

Heat olive oil in large Dutch oven. Saute onion, garlic, celery, parsley and basil 5 minutes, stirring often. Sprinkle sugar over mixture and stir. Add beef stock and water; bring to a boil. Reduce heat to medium. Add remaining ingredients except macaroni and Parmesan cheese. Cook 35 minutes. Add macaroni and cook 35 minutes more, stirring occasionally. Sprinkle with freshly grated Parmesan cheese on each serving. Serve with bread stick or garlic bread.

"I got this recipe from Nancy A. Dayak."

Jackie Rupp   **Home Street Middle School, Bishop, CA**

GRANDMA'S MINESTRONE SOUP

Serves 6 - 8

½ pound salt pork, ground
1 ½ onions, chopped
4 cloves garlic, chopped
few sprigs of parsley, freshly minced
4 quarts water
½ head green cabbage, chopped
2 bundles Swiss chard, cut up
1 pound fresh Italian flat beans
1 can kidney beans, mashed
4 (medium) zucchini, sliced
1 ¼ pound fresh peas
½ teaspoon salt
½ teaspoon pepper
½ teaspoon oregano
½ teaspoon celery salt
3 potatoes, diced
1 bundle fresh basil, chopped
6 ounces macaroni

Garnish: Parmesan cheese, grated, to taste

Easy Italian Favorites

Brown ground pork in saucepan. Add onion, garlic and parsley to pork. Add water; bring to a boil and simmer slowly. Add cabbage, Swiss chard, flat beans, mashed kidney beans, zucchini, fresh peas, salt, pepper, oregano, celery salt, and potatoes; simmer until all vegetables are tender. Add basil and macaroni; cook until macaroni is tender. When ready to serve, add Parmesan cheese.

"Joyce Gibson's Italian mother-in-law, Irene Picollo, has had this recipe in her family for over four generations. Truly a traditional Italian recipe."

Mary Springhorn   **Anderson High School, Anderson, CA**

HAMBURGER-VEGETABLE SOUP

Serves 4

- 1 pound ground beef
- 6 cups water
- 1/2 teaspoon salt
- 1/4 teaspoon pepper
- 1/4 teaspoon oregano
- 1/4 teaspoon basil
- 1 package onion soup mix
- 1 (8 ounce) can tomato sauce
- 1 tablespoon soy sauce
- 3 to 4 stalks celery, sliced
- 3 carrots, sliced
- 1/2 cup dried split peas
- 1 cup macaroni
- *Garnish:* Parmesan cheese, grated

Brown ground beef; drain excess grease. Add water, salt, pepper, oregano, basil, onion soup mix, tomato sauce and soy sauce. Bring to a boil; simmer 15 minutes. Add celery, carrots and split peas, simmer 30 minutes or more. Add macaroni and continue simmering 15 minutes, until done. Serve with grated Parmesan cheese. NOTE: Before serving, add more water to thin soup, if necessary.

"This soup is a main dish that my grandfather used to make for me. It's still popular with my family and my students."

Peggy Elder   **Mt. Carmel High School, San Diego, CA**

ITALIAN CAESAR DRESSING

Makes 1 cup

- 1/2 cup olive oil
- 2 tablespoons red wine vinegar
- 2 tablespoons lemon juice
- 1 tablespoon worcestershire sauce
- 1 teaspoon Dijon mustard
- 1 teaspoon lemon peel, grated
- 1 (large) clove garlic, minced
- 2 drops Tabasco sauce

Whisk all ingredients together in small bowl.

"This Caesar dressing is an oil and vinegar style instead of the classic creamy style."

Janet Tingley   **Atascadero High School, Atascadero, CA**

ITALIAN SALAD PIZZA
Serves 8

1 (10 ounce) package refrigerated pizza crust
2 cloves garlic, pressed
1 teaspoon dried oregano
$\frac{1}{2}$ teaspoon dried basil
Toppings:
$\frac{1}{2}$ cup red onion, thinly sliced
$\frac{1}{4}$ cup pitted ripe olives, sliced
1 (medium) tomato, chopped
5 cups romaine lettuce, thinly sliced
$\frac{1}{4}$ cup Italian dressing
1 cup mozzarella cheese, shredded
$\frac{1}{4}$ to $\frac{1}{2}$ cup Parmesan cheese, grated

Preheat oven to 425 degrees. Roll out pizza crust to fit a 15" pizza pan or stone. Press garlic over dough and spread evenly. Sprinkle oregano and basil over dough. Bake on bottom rack for 12 to 14 minutes or until crust is golden brown. While crust bakes, prepare toppings. Place toppings in a 2 quart bowl and toss with dressing. When crust is done, immediately top it with mozzarella and half of the Parmesan cheese. Add salad mixture and remaining Parmesan cheese. Serve immediately.

Nicole Rehmann   **La Mesa Junior High School, Santa Clarita, CA**

ITALIAN SAUSAGE SOUP
Serves 10

12 mild or hot Italian sausage
1 onion, chopped
3 cloves garlic, crushed
$\frac{1}{2}$ cup dry wine
4 cups broth
1 (large) can crushed tomatoes
2 to 3 zucchini, cut into $\frac{1}{4}$" slices
1 bell pepper, chopped
1 cup pasta shells, uncooked
3 teaspoons Italian herbs
4 tablespoons parsley
salt, to taste

Cut sausage into $\frac{1}{4}$" slices and brown in Dutch oven. Remove meat to side and discard saturated fat. Saute chopped onion and garlic in pan until tender. Add wine, broth, tomatoes, zucchini, bell pepper, pasta, sausage, herbs and parsley. Season to taste with salt. Simmer 30 minutes or longer, until pasta is cooked.

"We love this recipe. It's easy, and it's a balanced meal in itself. I suggest sprinkling each bowl with Parmesan or Romano cheese when serving."

Deborah Scott-Toux   **Eisenhower High School, Rialto, CA**

KILLER PASTA SALAD

Serves 8 - 10

Dressing:
1 tablespoon Dijon mustard
5 cloves garlic, chopped
$\frac{1}{4}$ cup white wine vinegar
$\frac{3}{4}$ cup olive oil
$\frac{1}{4}$ cup green onion, (both green and white parts) chopped
salt and freshly ground pepper, to taste

Salad:
$\frac{1}{4}$ cup snow peas, fresh or frozen
1 (small) bunch broccoli florets, cut into small pieces
2 (small) zucchini, cut into $\frac{1}{4}$" slices
1 (large) red bell pepper, seeded, cut into thin strips
1 pound short pasta (rotelle, fusilli, penne)
$\frac{1}{4}$ cup Parmesan or Asiago cheese, freshly grated

Dressing: Combine ingredients in a blender and blend until creamy; set aside.
Salad: Cook snow peas in boiling water for 1 minute. Remove and drench with cold water. Repeat with broccoli and zucchini, cooking 3 minutes each. Combine cooked veggies in a bowl with red bell pepper. Toss with half of the dressing. Add pasta and toss. Sprinkle with grated cheese. NOTE: You can add blanched carrots and cold tomatoes to increase the nutrition and give more color. You can also substitute yellow or orange bell pepper for the red pepper.

"This is a good accompaniment to grilled meats.
Add cold chicken, shrimp or beef for a refreshing dinner pasta salad."

Marty Parker   **Poway High School, Poway, CA**

MINUTE LAMB MINESTRONE

Serves 6   *Photo opposite page 33*

1 (16 ounce) package seasoned frozen pasta and vegetable mix
(such as Green Giant's Pasta Accents mixes;
Garden Herb Seasoning or Garlic Seasoning)
4 $\frac{1}{2}$ cups reduced salt beef broth
1 (14.5 ounce) can diced tomatoes, or whole tomatoes, cut up
3 tablespoons tomato paste
1 (8.75 ounce) can kidney beans, drained
1 teaspoon Italian seasoning, crushed
1 $\frac{1}{2}$ cups American lamb, cooked, cut into small cubes
Pesto, optional

In a large saucepan, combine pasta/vegetable mix and beef broth. Bring to a boil; reduce heat. Cover and simmer 5 minutes. Stir in tomatoes, tomato paste, kidney beans, Italian seasoning and lamb. Bring to a boil; cook 1 minute to heat through. Serve with a dollop of pesto, if desired.

American Sheep industry   **Englewood, CO**

PESTO FETA PASTA SALAD
Serves 8 - 10

1 pound rotini pasta
1 (small) jar sun dried tomatoes
1 (small) can olives, pitted, drained
1 jar artichoke hearts, drained
½ cup feta or jack cheese, grated
1 bottle Trader Joe's Basil & Garlic Dressing
1 container Trader Joe's pesto
salt and pepper, to taste

Boil rotini according to package directions; rinse and drain well. Place pasta in large salad bowl. Add tomatoes, olives, artichokes hearts and grated cheese. Pour dressing and pesto over pasta. Season to taste. Toss well and chill. Serve cold.

Reiko Ikkanda   **So. Pasadena Middle School, So. Pasadena, CA**

PIZZA SOUP
Serves 4

1 ¼ cup fresh mushrooms, sliced
½ cup onion, finely chopped
1 teaspoon vegetable oil
2 cups water
1 (15 ounce) can pizza sauce
1 cup pepperoni, chopped
1 cup fresh tomatoes, chopped
½ cup Italian sausage, cooked
¼ teaspoon Italian seasoning
¼ cup Parmesan cheese, grated
Garnish: mozzarella cheese, shredded

In a large saucepan, saute mushrooms and onion in oil for 2 to 3 minutes or until tender. Add water, pizza sauce, pepperoni, tomatoes, sausage and Italian seasoning. Bring to a boil over medium heat. Reduce heat; cover and simmer 20 minutes, stirring occasionally. Before serving, stir in Parmesan cheese. Garnish with mozzarella cheese.

Sally Reimers   **Sinaloa Middle School, Simi Valley, CA**

SAUSAGE & TORTELLINI SOUP
Serves 6 - 8

¼ to ½ pound mild Italian sausage
1 onion, chopped
2 cups zucchini, sliced
1 cup carrots, sliced
1 cup green pepper, cut into 1" squares
1 large clove garlic, chopped
¼ teaspoon dried oregano leaves, crushed
3 ½ cups chicken broth (fresh or canned)
3 ½ cups water
1 (8 ounce) can chopped tomatoes, undrained
1 cup parsley, chopped
1 (12 ounce) package frozen tortellini
Garnish: Freshly grated Parmesan cheese

Easy Italian Favorites

Remove the casing from the sausage; coarsely chop sausage and brown in skillet with onion, zucchini, carrots, green pepper, garlic and oregano. Add chicken broth, water, tomatoes and parsley; bring to a boil. Add tortellini and simmer 15 to 20 minutes or until pasta is tender. Serve with freshly grated Parmesan cheese.

Vicki Giannetti   **Foothill High School, Sacramento, CA**

SIMPLE PASTA SALAD
Serves 8

    2 cups pasta, uncooked
    2 cups fresh vegetables, cut into chunks (carrots, celery, peppers,
        broccoli, zucchini, mushrooms, green onions,
        cherry tomatoes, cucumbers, etc.)
    1 (8 ounce) bottle vinaigrette or Italian style salad dressing

Cook pasta in boiling water for 8 minutes. Drain well in a colander. While pasta is cooking, chop vegetables into bite-size chunks or a size that will fit with the size pasta you are using. Add vegetables and salad dressing to warm, drained pasta in large plastic container with a lid and mix well. Serve immediately or refrigerate (which increases the flavor) 2 to 24 hours before serving. NOTE: Vegetables of different colors and amounts of crunchiness will improve the overall result. If you are using any vegetables that you prefer cooked instead of raw, steam, parboil or microwave those briefly before adding to the pasta. Frozen vegetables won't taste like fresh, but a bag of stir-fry style vegetables works well and is convenient. Defrost and drain before adding to pasta but don't cook the vegetables. Adding the vegetables and dressing to the pasta while it's warm helps the flavors blend together. You can also add strips of salami and cubes of cheese.

"I put this recipe together in a hurry one day when I had about 5 hours notice to provide dinner at a professional group's Board meeting for 14 women that evening."

Nancy Murray   **El Capitan High School, Lakeside, CA**

SPAGHETTI SALAD
Serves 12

    1 pound spaghetti, cooked, cooled
    1 green bell pepper, diced
    1 cucumber, peeled, diced
    2 (large) tomatoes, diced
    1 (large) red onion, diced
    1 (small) can black olives, sliced, drained
    1 bottle Italian dressing
    1 tablespoon Schilling Salad Supreme
    salt and garlic powder to taste
    dash Tabasco sauce

Combine cooled spaghetti with vegetables; toss well with dressing. Add seasonings and Tabasco to taste. Refrigerate several hours or overnight.

"This recipe is a student favorite at our salad buffet lab."

Wanda Shelton   **Newport Harbor High School, Newport Harbor, CA**

Spinach & Tortellini Soup
Serves 10 - 12

3 (large) cans chicken broth
1 (8 ounce) package fresh cheese-filled spinach tortellini
1 bunch (¾ pound) fresh spinach
4 boneless, skinless chicken breasts, cut into 2" chunks
½ pound mushrooms
1 cup rice, cooked
2 teaspoons dry tarragon leaves
ground pepper, to taste
Garnish: Parmesan cheese, grated

Put broth into a large pot and bring to a boil. Add tortellini and boil gently for 6 to 8 minutes, uncovered. Wash spinach; discard tough leaves; chop remaining leaves. Add chopped spinach, chicken chunks, mushrooms, rice and tarragon to broth. Bring to a boil over high heat for 2 to 3 minutes. Add pepper. Serve with grated Parmesan cheese.

"Recipe from my sister, Steph. Tastes great with a tossed green salad and French bread."
Susan Lefler   **Ramona Junior High School, Chino, CA**

Summer Garden Pasta
Serves 4

8 ounces corkscrew pasta
⅓ cup olive oil
3 (medium) zucchini, thinly sliced
1 cup red onion, chopped
¼ cup Parmesan cheese, grated
¼ cup fresh basil, chopped
¼ cup fresh chives, chopped
¼ cup fresh parsley, chopped
2 (medium) tomatoes, cut into wedges or 8 cherry tomatoes, halved
½ teaspoon salt
½ teaspoon pepper
2 tablespoons lemon juice

Cook pasta according to package directions; drain. Meanwhile, in large skillet over medium heat, heat oil. Add zucchini and onion and cook 5 minutes, until zucchini is crisp-tender, stirring occasionally. Add remaining ingredients; cover and cook just until tomatoes are heated through. Add hot pasta, tossing gently to mix well. NOTE: Can be served warm or cold.

"This recipe came from a Women's Day Recipe Magazine."
Ruth Anne Schroeder   **River City High School, West Sacramento, CA**

TANGY RED, GREEN & WHITE SALAD
Serves 6

- 1 bag mixed salad greens
- 2 green onions, thinly sliced
- 2 stalks celery, diced
- 1/2 red pepper, julienned
- 1/4 cup feta or mozzarella cheese
- 1/4 cup raspberry vinegarette
- 1/4 cup walnuts, chopped (optional)

Place salad greens in salad bowl. Toss in green onion, celery, red pepper and feta cheese or mozzarella cheese. Sprinkle with raspberry vinegarette and toss.

Bobbi Witten   **Fountain Valley High School, Fountain Valley, CA**

TORTELLINI ASPARAGUS TOSS
Serves 4   *Photo opposite page 32*

- 1/4 cup red wine vinegar
- 2 tablespoons olive oil
- 1 1/2 teaspoons lemon juice
- 1 teaspoon sugar
- 1 1/4 teaspoons Lawry's Garlic Salt
- 1 pound fresh asparagus, cut into 1/2" pieces
- 2 cups fresh spinach leaves, tightly packed
- 2 (9 ounce) packages small cheese-filled tortellini
- 1 cup red bell pepper, diced

In small bowl, combine vinegar, oil, lemon juice, sugar and garlic salt; set aside. Cook asparagus in microwave or steam on cook top in saucepan with small amount of water; remove asparagus to large bowl. Cook spinach in same dish or saucepan, just until wilted; add spinach to asparagus. In large pot, cook tortellini according to package directions in unsalted water; drain. Add tortellini to vegetables in bowl and pour dressing over all. Add red bell pepper and toss salad gently but thoroughly. May serve warm or chilled, as desired.

Variations: 1 1/2 cups broccoli florets can replace asparagus, diced pimientos, drained, can replace red bell pepper.

Lawry's Foods, Inc.   **Monrovia, CA**

ZESTY ITALIAN PASTA SALAD
Serves 10 - 12

- 1 (12 ounce) package rotelle or spaghetti
- 1 cup carrots, sliced
- 1/2 cup green onion, chopped
- 1/2 cup olives, sliced
- 1 cup broccoli crowns, chopped (optional)
- 1 (16 ounce) bottle zesty Italian dressing
- salt and pepper, to taste
- Salad Supreme Seasoning, to taste

Cook rotelle or spaghetti according to package directions; rinse and drain. Add carrots, green onion, olives and broccoli, if using. Pour bottled dressing over and toss. Add salt, pepper and Salad Supreme to taste. Chill 2 to 3 hours before serving.

Karol Meryhew   **Granger High School, West Valley, UT**

Side Dishes

CREAMY RISOTTO
Serves 4 - 6

6 tablespoons butter, divided
1 (small) onion, chopped
1 clove garlic, minced
2 cups arborio rice
salt and pepper, to taste
pinch saffron
5 $\frac{1}{2}$ cups chicken broth
$\frac{1}{2}$ cup dry white wine
$\frac{3}{4}$ cup Parmesan cheese, grated

In large stockpot, melt 2 tablespoons butter. Add onions and garlic and saute until translucent. Add rice, salt, pepper, saffron; saute lightly. In a medium saucepan, heat broth and keep at a simmer. Add wine to rice and cook until liquid has evaporated. Add 1 cup hot chicken broth and cook, stirring occasionally over low heat until all of the liquid is absorbed. Add more broth, gradually, and cook while stirring until it is absorbed. Continue cooking the rice, adding more broth every 3 to 4 minutes until each broth addition is absorbed. When all the broth has been added and absorbed, after about 25 minutes, stir in remaining butter and Parmesan cheese. Risotto should be rich and creamy.

"This is delicious and rich! Students love it, and it is worth the extra effort."
Patti Bartholomew   **Casa Roble High School, Orangevale, CA**

FETTUCCINI WITH TOMATOES & ARTICHOKE HEARTS
Serves 4 - 6

1 envelope Good Seasons Italian dressing mix
$\frac{1}{4}$ cup olive oil
1 pound fresh tomatoes, diced
1 can artichoke hearts, drained, chopped
1 package fresh Contadina fettuccini

Mix Good Seasons dressing mix with olive oil in small bowl; stir in tomatoes and artichokes and marinate at least 1 hour. Cook fettuccini according to package directions. Drain and toss marinated mixture.

"This is very quick and easy when you need a quick side dish."
Karin Hitchen   **Arroyo Grande High School, Arroyo Grande, CA**

Fresh Green Beans Italiano
Serves 4

    1 pound fresh green beans
    2 tablespoons olive oil
    2 cloves garlic, minced
    salt and pepper, to taste

Clean the green beans and snap off the ends. In a medium saucepan, over high heat, bring salted water to a boil. Add the green beans. Blanch until beans are bright green, approximately 5 minutes. Combine olive oil and garlic in a serving bowl and set aside. Remove beans from heat; drain and rinse with cold water to stop further cooking. Toss beans with olive oil and garlic. Season with salt and pepper. Set aside to allow flavors to blend. Serve at room temperature.

"This is a great summer vegetable dish that can be prepared in advance."
Myrna Swearingen　　　　　　　　**Corona High School, Corona, CA**

Gnocchi
Serves 4 - 6

    7 (small) potatoes, peeled, cooked
    1 egg
    2 to 2 ½ cups flour
    4 quarts unsalted water
    pasta sauce

Peel and boil potatoes; drain and mash. Cool slightly. Add egg and flour to form a soft dough. With hands, make a rope about ½" in diameter. Cut into ½" to ¾" pieces. Place on a lightly floured surface to dry 2 to 3 hours. Bring water to a boil. Cook in boiling water to which a bit of oil has been added until they sink! Drain and serve with your favorite pasta sauce.

"My grandma used to roll the cut pieces against the side of a grater to make them look fancy! I am still working at making mine taste as good as my mom's!"
Maria Fregulia　　　　　　　　**Lassen High School, Susanville, CA**

Italian Vegetable Bake
Serves 6

    3 to 4 zucchini, thickly sliced
    3 to 4 yellow crookneck squash, thickly sliced
    2 to 3 tomatoes, cut into wedges
    1 onion, thinly sliced
    2 teaspoons Italian seasoning mix or basil and salt
    2 to 4 tablespoons oil
    Garnish: Parmesan cheese, grated (optional)

Place zucchini and yellow squash slices in a 9" x 13" casserole dish. Add tomatoes and onion. Sprinkle with Italian seasoning or basil and salt. Drizzle with olive oil. Bake at 350 degrees 20 minutes (if at room temperature, up to 30 minutes if refrigerated ahead of cooking). Cook until vegetables are tender. Sprinkle with Parmesan cheese, if desired

"Very colorful, nutritious, quick and easy. Vegetables may be layered, arranged or mixed. It is best if casserole dish can also be the serving dish."
Janet Riness　　　　　　　　**Westminster High School, Westminster, CA**

Tortellini Asparagus Toss
Everyone loves this attractive salad.
(page 30)

Minute Lamb Minestrone
A quick complete meal.
(page 26)

OVEN FRIES ITALIANO
Serves 4

4 large all-purpose potatoes (about 2 pounds) unpeeled
1 tablespoon butter
1 tablespoon olive oil
2 cloves garlic, minced
3/4 teaspoon basil
3/4 teaspoon oregano
1/2 teaspoon salt
1/4 teaspoon pepper
1/4 cup Parmesan cheese, grated

Preheat oven to 425 degrees. Line a baking sheet with foil and lightly grease the foil. Cut potatoes lengthwise into 1/2" thick wedges. Melt butter and combine with oil, garlic, and spices in a large bowl. Add potatoes and toss to coat well with herbed butter. Arrange potatoes on baking sheet and sprinkle evenly with Parmesan. Bake 30 minutes or until tender and golden. Twice during cooking, use spatula to turn potatoes and ensure even cooking.

"These make a nice accompaniment to your favorite barbecued burgers or steaks."
Penny Niadna   **Golden West High School, Visalia, CA**

PARMESAN CRISPS
Serves 4

1 cup Parmesan or Romano cheese, freshly grated

Preheat oven to 350 degrees. Place 1/4 cup grated cheese in piles on an ungreased baking sheet. Spread out to make flat rounds. Bake 6 minutes, or until edges are brown. Cool 3 minutes, then remove from pan.

"These go great with a main dish salad or soup."
Diane Field   **Dinuba High School, Dinuba, CA**

PASTA & TOMATOES WITH A BITE
Serves 6

12 ounce package egg noodles
1/4 cup olive oil
1 dried red chili or 1 tablespoon crushed red chili flakes
1 teaspoon dried basil
1 teaspoon dried oregano
1 teaspoon parsley
2 cloves garlic, minced
1 (16 ounce) can stewed, diced tomatoes

Cook noodles according to package directions; drain. Meanwhile, in olive oil, saute chili pepper flakes, basil, oregano, parsley and garlic. Add tomatoes and heat through. Toss sauce with noodles and serve.

Monica Blanchette   **Landmark Middle School, Moreno Valley, CA**

Quick Polenta
Serves 6

- 1 ½ quarts water
- 2 teaspoon salt
- 2 cups instant polenta
- 3 tablespoons butter
- ½ teaspoon pepper
- ½ cup Parmesan cheese, grated

In large saucepan, bring water and salt to a boil over high heat. Stir in polenta in a slow steady stream. Reduce heat to medium and continue stirring 5 minutes, or until polenta is thickened to consistency of hot cereal. Remove polenta from heat and stir in butter, pepper and Parmesan cheese.

"My vegetarian daughter keeps a package of polenta at our house so she'll always have something to eat when she comes for a visit."

Kathy Warren   **C.K. McClatchy High School, Sacramento, CA**

Ratatouille on the Run
Serves 4

- 2 tablespoons olive oil
- 4 (large) cloves garlic, chopped
- 1 (large) eggplant, unpeeled, diced
- 2 green bell peppers, diced
- 2 large tomatoes, chopped
- 1 onion, cut into 1" pieces
- 1 (large) zucchini, cut into ½" pieces
- ½ cup fresh basil, chopped or 1 tablespoon dried
- 2 tablespoons red wine vinegar
- salt and pepper, to taste
- 4 ounces goat or Muenster cheese, or a mixture of both, diced

Heat oil in heavy Dutch over over medium heat. Add garlic, stir 1 minute. Add eggplant, bell peppers, tomatoes, onion, zucchini and basil. Saute 5 minutes. Cover and simmer until all vegetables are tender, stirring occasionally, about 25 minutes. Preheat oven to 350 degrees. Uncover pot and simmer until juice thickens, stirring occasionally, about 10 minutes. Mix in vinegar, season to taste with salt and pepper. Spread ratatouille in a 9" pie dish. Sprinkle with cheese, if desired, and heat until cheese melts.

"A really quick dish in the summer to use up all the fresh vegetables in your garden."

Julie Shelburne   **Tulare Union High School, Tulare, CA**

Sauteed Zucchini
Serves 4

- 2 tablespoons olive oil
- 2 zucchini, sliced
- 3 mushrooms, sliced
- 1 clove garlic, minced
- *Garnish:* Parmesan cheese, grated

Heat olive oil over medium heat; add zucchini, mushrooms and garlic. Saute until al dente. Sprinkle with Parmesan cheese and serve.

Carol Steele   **Arroyo Seco Junior High School, Valencia, CA**

Spaghetti with Garlic Sauce
Serves 4

1 pound spaghetti, cooked
½ cup butter
½ cup olive oil
4 (small) cloves garlic, minced
2 tablespoons fresh parsley, chopped
Garnish: Parmesan cheese, grated

Prepare spaghetti according to package directions. Meanwhile, melt butter in a large pan. Add olive oil. Saute minced garlic in oil until golden brown. Add cooked spaghetti and parsley. Cook over low heat until heated through. Serve with grated Parmesan cheese.

"My husband's favorite, from his Italian mother."

Pat Smith   **Kern Valley High School, Lake Isabella, CA**

Spicy Pasta Alfredo Casserole
Serves 6 - 10

1 (12 ounce) package fettuccini
2 (1.6 ounce) package Alfredo sauce mix
2 cups milk
1 cup water
2 tablespoons butter
1 (16 ounce) carton sour cream
1 (10 ounce) can diced tomatoes & green chiles, drained
1 (14 ounce) jar artichoke hearts, drained, quartered
1 (12 ounce) jar roasted red peppers, drained, chopped
1 cup Parmesan cheese, shredded

Cook pasta according to package instructions; drain well and set aside. Combine sauce mix and next 3 ingredients in a large saucepan; bring to a boil, stirring constantly. Reduce heat and cook until thick and bubbly. Stir in sour cream and tomatoes with green chiles. Combine pasta, sauce, artichoke and red peppers, Spoon into a greased 9" x 13" baking dish. Cover and bake at 350 degrees for 1 hour. Uncover, and sprinkle with Parmesan cheese. Bake 10 minutes more.

"Add some cooked diced chicken, and you have a great main dish!"

Connie Halloway   **Rubidoux High School, Riverside, CA**

Stewed Eggplant & Tomatoes
Serves 6

2 to 3 tablespoons olive oil
1 (large) onion, chopped
1 eggplant, cut into ½" cubes
2 (large) cans whole tomatoes
dash oregano
2 tablespoons parsley
¼ cup fresh basil, chopped
½ cup Italian cheese, grated

Coat large skillet with olive oil and saute onion and eggplant until slightly soft. Crush tomatoes by hand. Add tomatoes and remaining ingredients to skillet and simmer for about 1 hour. You may add more cheese, if desired.

Sandra Blair   **Turlock High School, Turlock, CA**

TONY'S PASTA & GREEN TOMATOES

Serves 4

> 4 cups pasta, cooked
> 4 (large) green tomatoes, thinly sliced (1/8" thick)
> salt and pepper, to taste
> 1 cup flour
> oil, for frying
> garlic
> cheese, grated

Prepare pasta according to package directions; drain well and set aside. Season tomatoes with salt and pepper. Coat with flour and fry in hot oil with garlic until golden brown. Do not overcook. Place fried tomato slices on top of hot, cooked pasta. Top with your favorite grated cheese and serve immediately!

"One of my favorite recipes! Enjoy!"

Kristine Carlin   **San Luis Obispo High School, San Luis Obispo, CA**

TORTA TERESA

Serves 6

> 1/4 cup extra virgin olive oil
> 2 bunches green onions, chopped
> 3 cloves garlic, minced
> 3 cups rice, cooked
> 6 eggs, beaten
> 1 cup spinach, cooked
> 1/4 cup Parmesan cheese, grated
> plain bread crumbs

Heat oil in large skillet over medium heat. Add green onion and garlic; cook until tender. Remove from heat and stir in rice and eggs; mix well. Stir in spinach and cheese. Coat a greased 9" x 12" glass baking dish with bread crumbs. Pour in rice mixture. Bake at 400 degrees 45 minutes, until set. Cool. Cut into diamond shaped pieces and serve warm or cold.

Variation: You can substitute 4 cups thinly sliced or grated zucchini for the spinach. Cook zucchini with onion and garlic. Add 1 1/2 cups ricotta cheese with eggs. Bake at 375 degrees about 1 hour.

Jean Adams   **Sonora High School, Sonora, CA**

VEGETABLE MARINADE
Serves 10 - 12

3 bunches broccoli
1 head cauliflower
10 to 12 carrots
1 pound mushrooms
Marinade:
1 cup seasoned gourmet rice vinegar
1 ½ cups extra-virgin olive oil
2 tablespoons dill weed
1 teaspoon salt
6 cloves garlic, sliced
1 tablespoon sugar

Clean and cut broccoli and cauliflower into bite-size florets. Clean and cut carrots approximately ¼" circles with a crinkle cutter. Clean but do not cut mushrooms. Mix together vinegar, olive oil, dill weed, salt, garlic and sugar. Place vegetables in large container that can be sealed. Pour marinade over all. Seal with lid and shake well. Refrigerate overnight. In the morning, shake container well and place back in refrigerator. Take vegetables out of marinade and display in glass bowl for serving.

"This is my son's favorite dish. It is perfect for buffets, church dinners, picnics or dinner parties. Everyone will love it! Don't plan on bringing any home!"

Toni Carnes   **Exeter High School, Exeter, CA**

---

*Olive oil has been found to be one of the best oils for you.
Garlic is said to have many health benefits.
Italian recipes usually use a lot of both!*

Jane Souza   **No. Monterey Co. HS, Castroville, CA**

AWESOME PIZZA DOUGH FROM SCRATCH
Makes 1 large crust

> 1 cup + 2 tablespoons water
> 1 package dry active yeast or 2 $\frac{1}{4}$ teaspoons
> 1 tablespoon sugar
> 1 $\frac{1}{2}$ teaspoons salt
> 1 $\frac{1}{2}$ tablespoons oil
> 2 $\frac{3}{4}$ to 3 $\frac{1}{4}$ cups unsifted flour
> 1 teaspoon cornmeal

Using your largest mixing bowl, stir yeast into warm water; add sugar, salt and oil. Stir just until mixed and yeast, sugar and salt are dissolved. Stir in 1 cup flour. Beat with a large spoon, about 100 strokes. Gradually stir in more flour, gently mixing with hands until no longer sticky. Turn dough out onto counter or bread board or pastry cloth and knead as one piece, 8 to 10 minutes. Cover dough with a clean towel and let it rest for about 10 minutes. Preheat oven to 425 degrees. Lightly grease a cookie sheet or pizza pan, sprinkle with cornmeal. Roll out dough to shape of pan on counter or in the pan. Slightly roll the edges. Bake 10 minutes, then remove from oven and top as desired. Bake 1 to 2 minutes more, until edges are golden brown. NOTE; To prepare this ahead: After dough rests, put dough in large ziploc bag and freeze overnight. When ready to use, remove from freezer and thaw completely, allowing dough to rise again (2 to 3 hours).

"This is actually a French bread recipe, so we used it first to bake bread, then pizza. It's the best pizza dough recipe I've found in 20 years of pizzas!"

Julie Hampton   **Gresham High School, Gresham, OR**

CHEESY GARLIC BREAD
Serves 6 - 8

> $\frac{1}{2}$ cup mayonnaise
> 1 cube margarine, softened
> $\frac{1}{2}$ cup cheese, grated
> 2 green onions, finely chopped
> 1 loaf French bread
> garlic salt, to taste
> Salad Supreme seasoning, to taste

Combine first 4 ingredients thoroughly. Slice French bread lengthwise. Spread with butter mixture. Sprinkle lightly with garlic salt and Salad Supreme. Broil in oven until melted and bubbly. Cut into serving pieces.

"Delicious with a tossed salad or soup."

Carol Winter   **Hillcrest High School, Midvale, UT**

Egg Noodles

Serves 4 - 6

1 1/4 cups flour
1/2 teaspoon salt
1 egg yolk
1 egg
1/4 cup water
extra flour, for dusting
large pot boiling water

In a large bowl, mix flour and salt. In a small bowl, mix egg yolk, egg and water. Make a well in the flour and add egg mixture; mix thoroughly until a stiff dough forms. Place dough on a floured surface and knead 10 minutes. Bring a large stock pot of water to a boil. On floured surface, roll out dough very thin; cut into strips. Place all noodles into boiling water and cook 10 to 15 minutes. Drain in colander and serve with desired sauce.

"These noodles can be served with spaghetti, Alfredo or butter sauce."

Patty Stroming   **Mitchell Sr. Elementary, Atwater, CA**

Garlic Toast

Makes 12 pieces

6 hot dog buns
1/4 cup margarine
2 cloves garlic, minced
2 tablespoons Parmesan cheese, grated (optional)
1 teaspoon paprika
2 tablespoons dried parsley flakes

Preheat broiler. Open buns and place, cut side up on cookie sheet. Melt butter in custard cup in microwave oven, about 45 seconds. Add garlic, then brush on tops of buns. Sprinkle with Parmesan cheese, if using. In diagonal rows, alternate stripes of paprika and parsley. Place under broiler and watch carefully. Should only take 1 to 2 minutes or become golden brown. Place in a napkin-lined basket to serve.

"This is a favorite lab of my students."

Sue Ogden   **San Clemente High School, San Clemente, CA**

Gorgonzola Focaccia

Makes Two 9" loaves

Dough:
3 1/2 teaspoons active dry yeast
1 1/2 cups warm water
1/4 cup olive oil
3 3/4 cups unbleached all-purpose flour
2 1/2 teaspoons salt
Topping:
8 ounces Gorgonzola cheese
1/4 cup whipping cream
1/2 teaspoon dried thyme
olive oil, for brushing tops

Dough: Stir yeast into warm water in large mixing bowl. Let stand 10 minutes. Stir in oil, then flour and salt. Knead on lightly floured surface until smooth and elastic, 8 to 10 minutes. Place dough in an oiled bowl, cover tightly and let rise until doubled, 1 to 1 ½ hours. Cut dough in half and place each piece in a lightly oiled 9" to 10" pie plate. Flatten and stretch dough to cover as much of the bottom as possible, then dimple tops quite vigorously with fingertips to stretch some more. Cover with a towel and let dough relax 10 minutes. Dimple and stretch again so that it really covers the bottom. Let rest once more for 20 to 25 minutes.

Topping: Mash cheese in a bowl with a wooden spoon and beat in cream and thyme. Spread cheese mixture equally over the doughs. Brush the tops lightly with olive oil and cover with a towel; let rise until well puffed, 50 to 60 minutes. Heat oven to 425 degrees. Bake 10 minutes; reduce heat to 375 degrees and bake until topping is golden brown and just starting to bubble, about 10 minutes. Unmold immediately.

"A savory treat that is appealing to the eye and tastebuds! The cheese settles into the valleys creating an uneven, rustic surface. Best when eaten slightly warm."
Toni Morucci   **Pleasant Valley High School, Chico, CA**

HOMEMADE TOMATO & BASIL PASTA
Serves 4

- 1 cup all purpose flour
- 1 large egg
- 1 tablespoon tomato paste
- 1 teaspoon dried basil or 1 tablespoon fresh basil
- 2 tablespoons water

Fill large saucepan full of water and bring to a boil over high heat. Meanwhile, mound flour in a large bowl and make a deep well in center. Break egg into a liquid measuring cup. Add tomato paste, basil and water and mix together with egg beater. Pour egg mixture in well. Using fork in a circular motion, stir until dough forms. Lightly flour cutting board and knead dough for one or two minutes. Divide dough into four pieces. With a rolling pin, roll out one fourth of the dough into a rectangle about 1/16" thick. (If dough is sticky, turn and flour both sides as you roll.) Roll dough into a strip and transfer to a lightly floured surface or cloth; leave uncovered while you roll out the remaining portions. Let each strip dry for 5 to 10 minutes until it feels flexible like a chamois cloth. When all dough is rolled, cut each strip in half and cut into desired noodle shape. Cook noodles at once in boiling water for three minutes, or until al dente. Drain and serve with desired sauce.

"We also make Alfredo sauce for this beautiful rose colored pasta."
Sue Campbell   **Marsh Junior High School, Chico, CA**

INCREDIBLE GARLIC BREAD
Makes 1 loaf

- 1 (1pound) loaf frozen bread dough
- 1/4 cup butter or margarine
- 1 tablespoons fresh parsley, finely chopped
- 1 tablespoon beaten egg
- 1 teaspoon garlic powder

Thaw bread just until it can be sliced, about 30 minutes. Cut loaf into slices. (You can slice the bread again into lengthwise halves if you wish.) Keep pieces in loaf shape for easy reassembly. Grease a 9" x 5" loaf pan. Melt butter. Stir in parsley, egg and garlic powder. Dip bread dough pieces in butter mixture, coating completely. Reassemble loaf in the prepared pan. Pour any extra butter mixture on top. Let rise in a warm-draft free area until doubled, about 2 ½ hours. Bake at 350 degrees for about 25 minutes, or until top is golden brown. Let cool slightly in pan before serving.

"I make this 3 loaves at a time. Everyone just loves this super easy recipe. Be sure to put foil under the pan as the butter topping tends to drip and burn as the loaves bake. Enjoy!"
Laura May   **Hesperia Junior High School, Hesperia, CA**

ITALIAN BREAD
Makes 4 loaves
   3 cups warm water
   2 tablespoons yeast
   1 tablespoon salt
   2 tablespoons oil
   2 tablespoons sugar
   7 cups flour
   cornmeal
   1 egg white, beaten

Combine water, yeast, salt, oil and sugar in large bowl. Add 3 cups flour. Mix with electric mixter until smooth. Add remaining flour and knead 3 to 4 minutes. Let rise 1 hour in a greased bowl. Divide dough into 4 loaves and place on cookie sheet that has been greased and sprinkled with cornmeal. Make diagonal slits in top of bread, if desired. Brush with beaten egg white, if desired. Bake at 350 degrees 30 minutes.

"This is an easy, low-cost, low-calorie recipe that is great with any pasta dish."
Kathy Sandoz   **Mesa Junior High School, Mesa, AZ**

ITALIAN FOCACCIA
Makes 2 loaves
   2 ½ to 3 cups all-purpose or unbleached flour
   2 teaspoons sugar
   ¼ teaspoon salt
   1 package regular or quick-acting dry yeast
   ¼ cup + 1 tablespoon olive or vegetable oil, divided
   1 cup very warm water (120 to 130 degrees)
   2 tablespoons fresh herbs (such as basil,
       oregano or rosemary) chopped
   2 tablespoons Parmesan cheese, grated
   2 tablespoons onion, chopped

Mix 1 cup flour, sugar, salt and yeast in a large bowl. Add ¼ cup oil and warm water. Beat on medium speed 3 minutes, scraping bowl occasionally. Stir in enough remaining flour until dough is soft and leaves side of bowl. Turn dough onto lightly floured surface; gently roll in flour to coat. Knead 5 to 10 minutes or until dough is smooth and elastic. Place in greased bowl; turn greased side up. Cover and let rise in warm place 1 to 1 ½ hours or until doubled in size. (Dough is ready if indentation remains when touched.) Heat oven to 425 degrees. Grease 2 cookie sheets. Punch dough down and divide in half. Shape each half into flattened 12" rounds on cookie sheet. Cover and let rise in warm place 20 minutes. Prick centers and 1" from edge thoroughly with fork. Brush with oil. Sprinkle each with 1 tablespoon herbs, cheese and onions, Bake 12 to 15 minutes, or until golden brown. Serve warm.
Myrna Westmoreland   **Grace Davis High School, Modesto, CA**

PEPPERONI LOAF

Makes 1 loaf

2 loaves frozen bread dough
½ pound pepperoni, chopped
2 eggs, beaten
¾ pound cheese, grated

Preheat oven to 250 degrees. Defrost bread dough but do not let it rise. Pat bread dough into a rectangle. Mix pepperoni, cheese and eggs; put on dough and fold over, pinching ends together. Bake immediately, 20 minutes at 250 degrees, then increase temperature to 350 degrees and continue baking 30 minutes more.

Debi Spencer   **Colton High School, Colton, CA**

When using fresh herbs, add toward the end of cooking time. Cooking pasta: 2 ounces pasta = 1 serving. 4 servings need at least 2 to 3 quarts boiling water with 1 tablespoon salt. Add pasta to boiling water, stirring gently until spaghetti softens and bends in the water. Let water come back to a boil and stir occasionally so pasta won't stick. Cook until al dente (or until done to your likeness). Drain pasta. DO NOT RINSE! This will take off the starch and the sauce won't cling to it.

JoAnn Himmelberger   **Santa Ana HS, Santa Ana, CA**

Sauces

BETSY'S MARINARA SAUCE
Makes 3 cups
- 1 (35 ounce) can plum tomatoes
- 1 (large) onion, diced
- 1 (large) carrot, diced
- 2 (large) cloves garlic, minced
- 1/4 cup olive oil
- 1 teaspoon basil, crushed
- 1/4 cup parsley
- 2 teaspoons salt, or to taste

Simmer tomatoes, onion and carrots for 15 minutes. Puree in blender and return to saucepan. Saute garlic in oil for 1 minute. Add to tomatoes and cook 5 minutes more. Stir in basil, parsley, and salt just before serving. Serve over cooked pasta.

"This is my personal favorite from my friend, Betsy Neil."

Dotti Jones   **Etiwanda High School, Etiwanda, CA**

CHUNKY SPAGHETTI SAUCE
Serves 10
- 1 pound ground beef
- 1 pound sweet Italian sausage
- 2 onions, chopped
- 2 cloves garlic, minced
- 1 bell pepper, chopped
- 1 pound fresh mushrooms, sliced
- 1 can olives, chopped
- 1 (large) can tomato paste
- 1 (large) can whole tomatoes
- 2 bay leaves
- Italian seasoning, to taste
- 1/2 cup sugar

Brown ground beef and half of the Italian sausage along with onion, garlic and bell pepper. Add mushrooms, olives, tomato paste and whole tomatoes. Simmer over very low heat 12 to 24 hours. 4 hours before serving, brown remaining Italian sausage and add to sauce. 1 hour before serving, add bay leaves, Italian seasoning and sugar. Remove bay leaves before serving.

"This recipe was a big hit at a Boy Scout Spaghetti Dinner which served 300."

Faye Nielsen   **Rosemead High School, Rosemead, CA**
Debra Jamison   **Basic High School, Henderson , NV**

CLASSIC ALFREDO SAUCE

Serves 6

- 2 cups heavy cream
- 2 sticks unsalted butter
- 1 teaspoon salt
- 1/4 teaspoon pepper
- 1/2 teaspoon nutmeg (optional)
- 1 cup Parmesan cheese, grated
- 2 tablespoons fresh parsley, chopped

Heat cream over low heat; melt butter in cream, bringing almost to boiling. Whisk in seasonings. Before serving, stir in cheese. Sprinkle with fresh parsley.

Pat Freshour   **Foothill High School, Palo Cedro, CA**

CROCKPOT PASTA SAUCE WITH MEAT

Makes 4 quarts

- 2 pounds ground beef
- 2 yellow onions, chopped
- 3 cloves garlic, crushed
- 5 (28 ounce) cans whole tomatoes, well drained
- 1 (16 ounce) can tomato paste
- 2 (8 ounce) cans tomato sauce
- 2 teaspoons dried basil
- 2 teaspoons dried oregano
- 2 teaspoons sugar
- 2 teaspoons salt
- 1 teaspoon pepper

In a large frying pan, brown ground beef with onions and garlic. Place in a 5 to 6 quart crockpot. Put well drained tomatoes in blender or food processor and puree until smooth. Add to crockpot. Add remaining ingredients and stir well. Cook in crockpot 10 to12 hours on low heat.

"Given to me by my Grandma Jo. She was Italian and one of the best cooks. This is a basic sauce that freezes well"

Beth Guerrero   **Selma High School, Selma, CA**

DIANE TRAW'S EASY MARINARA SAUCE

Serves 6 - 8

- 4 cloves garlic, peeled, chopped
- 1/2 small white onion, chopped
- 3 tablespons olive oil
- 1 (28 ounce) can tomatoes, with liquid
- 1 teaspoon sugar
- 1/4 teaspoon salt
- 1/2 teaspoon dried oregano
- 2 teaspoons dried basil
- 1/4 teaspoon crushed red pepper
- dash cinnamon

In a medium saucepan, saute garlic and onion in olive oil until translucent. Add remaining ingredients and simmer 1 hour, stirring occasionally. Serve over pasta, chicken, veal or pizza.

Marianne Traw   **Ball Junior High School, Anaheim, CA**

GREAT MARINARA SAUCE

Serves 4

1/4 (large) onion, chopped
1/2 green pepper, chopped
1 carrot, chopped
1 rib celery, chopped
1 clove garlic, minced
1/4 cup olive oil
2 cups canned tomatoes, diced
1/3 cup tomato paste
1 1/2 teaspoons dried basil, crushed
1 teaspoon dried oregano, crushed
1/2 teaspoon thyme
1 teaspoon sugar
1 teaspoon salt
1/4 teaspoon pepper

In large skillet, saute onion, green pepper, carrot, celery and garlic in olive oil until tender. Stir in undrained tomatoes, tomato paste, basil, oregano, thyme, sugar, salt and pepper. Bring to a boil, reduce heat, cover and simmer about 30 minutes. If necessary, uncover the last 10 to 15 minutes to get the desired consistency. Stir occasionally while cooking. Serve over your favorite pasta.

Shauna Osborne   **Jordan High School, Salt Lake City, UT**

LEMON PASTA SAUCE

Serves 4

1 pound pasta
3/4 cup water
1 teaspoon Italian herb seasoning
4 cubes chicken bouillon
1 tablespoon oil
1 teaspoon garlic
1/4 cup lemon juice
1/2 teaspoon cornstarch
1 tablespoon Parmesan cheese, grated

Cook pasta according to package directions; drain and set aside. Mix water, seasoning, bouillon, oil, garlic, lemon juice and cornstarch in saucepan and heat until slightly thickened. Pour sauce over cooked pasta, toss and top with Parmesan cheese and serve.

"Try this with bay shrimp."

Shannon M. Farmer   **Central High School, Fresno, CA**

MS. PUCCI'S PESTO SAUCE

1/4 cup pine nuts or walnuts
2 cloves garlic, peeled
1/4 cup fresh parsley
1 cup fresh basil
1/3 cup olive oil
1/4 cup Parmesan cheese, grated
1/4 teaspoon salt
1/4 teaspoon pepper

Easy Italian Favorites

In a blender or food processor, chop nuts and garlic. Add half of the olive oil, basil and parsley and blend. Add remaining half and blend until smooth. Slowly add cheese, salt and pepper and blend until smooth. The finished sauce should be slightly runny.

"For a lowfat creamy pesto, melt nonfat cream cheese and add to pesto."
Alicia Pucci   **Kenilworth Junior High School, Petaluma, CA**

PENELOPE'S PIZZA SAUCE

2 (8 ounce) cans tomato sauce
$1/4$ cup Parmesan cheese, grated
$1/2$ teaspoon garlic
$1/2$ teaspoon oregano
$1/2$ cup tomatoes, chopped (optional)
$1/2$ cup onions, chopped(optional)

Mix tomato sauce with cheese, herbs, tomatoes and onions (if using) over medium heat, stirring occasionally so cheese will not stick to bottom. Simmer 10 to 15 minutes. Use on your favorite pizza crust.

Cheryl M. Moyle   **Olympus High School, Salt Lake City, UT**

QUICK BEEF SPAGHETTI SAUCE

Serves 5 - 6

1 pound ground beef
$1/2$ cup onion, chopped
1 clove garlic, chopped
$3/4$ teaspoon salt
$1/4$ teaspoon pepper
1 teaspoon Italian seasoning
4 large mushrooms, sliced (optional)
2 (14 ounce) cans stewed tomatoes, Italian style
2 (8 ounce) cans tomato sauce
$1/2$ cup water

Fry hamburger, onion, and garlic until browned. Add spices and mushrooms, if using. Unless you like chunky sauce, blend tomatoes in blender until smooth; add to ground beef mixture. Add tomato sauce. Use water to rinse out cans and add to meat mixture. Simmer $1/2$ to 1 hour and serve with your favorite pasta.

"So simple, so fast, so delicious! This is delicious as a base for home made lasagna too! "
Pam Cahill   **Eureka High School, Eureka, CA**
Diedre Goodnough   **Norwalk High School, Norwalk, CA**

QUICK SPICY SAUCE

Serves 2

1 small can tomato sauce
1 teaspoon crushed dried oregano
$1/4$ cup Parmesan cheese, grated
1 package Boboli pizza sauce (optional)
$1/2$ small can Ortega chiles, chopped

Combine all ingredients and simmer 10 minutes.

Catherine Diaz   **Exeter Union High School, Exeter, CA**

SPICY RED SAUCE
Serves 4

- 1 teaspoon olive oil
- 2 ounces Italian sausage, cooked
- $\frac{1}{4}$ cup onion, chopped
- 2 cloves garlic, minced
- 1 cup fresh mushrooms, sliced
- 1 cup green peppers, chopped
- 1 (28 ounce) can crushed tomatoes, undrained
- 2 tablespoons parsley, chopped
- 1 teaspoon oregano
- $\frac{1}{2}$ to 1 teaspoon crushed red pepper
- $\frac{1}{4}$ teaspoon black pepper

Heat oil in saucepan. Stir in cooked sausage, onion and garlic; cook until onion is tender. Add mushrooms and green pepper and cook until vegetables are tender. Add tomatoes and all spices to saucepan. Bring to a boil and cover, simmering for 30 minutes. Serve over your favorite hot, cooked pasta.

Carrie Vaughn   **Cypress High School, Cypress, CA**

TOMATO SAUCE
Serves 4

- 2 tablespoons olive oil
- $\frac{1}{2}$ cup onion, finely chopped
- 2 cloves garlic, minced
- 3 tablespoons tomato paste
- 1 teaspoon dried basil
- $\frac{1}{2}$ teaspoon salt
- freshly ground black pepper
- 1 tablespoon balsamic vinegar
- 2 cups Italian plum, whole pack, or diced tomatoes, not drained

Using a 2 to 3 quart enameled or stainless steel saucepan, heat olive oil until a light haze forms over it. Add onions and cook over moderate heat 7 to 8 minutes, or until they're soft but not browned. Add garlic and tomato paste and fry or cook in olive oil until it turns from red to light orange. Add basil, salt, pepper, vinegar and tomatoes. Reduce heat to very low and simmer, with pan partially covered, for about 40 minutes, stirring occasionally. Press sauce through a fine sieve or food mill into bowl or pan. Taste for seasoning and serve hot. NOTE: You may add chopped mushrooms, chopped bell peppers, grated cheese, Parmesan cheese, jalapeno rings, chopped green onions, finely diced fresh tomatoes, etc. Browned, cooked meat may be added to this sauce.

"This sauce is simple, delicious and may be used not only with spaghetti but with any of your favorite Italian recipes."

Joan Wayland   **Holmes Junior High School, Davis, CA**

WALNUT PESTO SAUCE
Serves 6 - 8

½ cup walnuts, chopped
5 cloves garlic, peeled
½ teaspoon salt
2 cups fresh sweet basil leaves
⅓ cup olive oil
⅓ cup Parmesan cheese, grated
⅓ cup Romano cheese, grated
¼ pound butter, softened

In a blender, at high speed, pulverize the walnuts, garlic, salt and basil, stopping motor and scraping down jar with a spatula a few times to process ingredients evenly. When mixture is a thick paste, add the olive oil, a drop at a time, while the blender is running, until sauce is thick and creamy. Transfer to a mixing bowl and beat in cheese with a wooden spoon. Add butter and beat until smooth. Refrigerate in a tightly covered container until ready to use.

"A variation of the traditional pesto recipe; walnuts instead of the usual pine nuts. You can make this ahead of time too!"

Christine Whipp   **West Torrance High School, Torrance, CA**

ZESTY TOMATO SAUCE
Serves 6 - 8

4 (number 2) cans tomatoes
¼ cup olive oil
2 (large) onions, minced
2 cloves garlic, minced
2 tablespoons tomato paste
½ teaspoon thyme
½ teaspoon cumin
1 teaspoon oregano
½ teaspoon chili powder
1 (small) bay leaf
1 teaspoon salt
¼ teaspoon pepper
1 teaspoon sugar
½ teaspoon Worcestershire sauce
¼ teaspoon Tabasco

Pour tomatoes into large, heavy kettle; simmer. In heavy skillet, heat olive oil and fry onion and garlic until clear and light yellow. Add tomato paste, thyme, cumin and oregano. Heat, stirring occasionally until sauce mellows, about 10 minutes. Pour into simmering tomatoes. Add chili powder, bay leaf, salt, pepper and sugar. Simmer 2 hours, stirring occasionally. During last hour of cooking, add Worcestershire and Tabasco. Taste and adjust seasonings.

"Serve this sauce with meatballs over spaghetti, topped with grated Parmesan or Provolone cheese. You may store extra sauce in freezer."

Judy Dobkins   **Redlands High School, Redlands, CA**

Pizza

ARTICHOKE-PEPPER PIZZA & FETA CHEESE

Serves 4 - 6

1 teaspoon olive oil
1 (small) red bell pepper, julienned
1 (small) yellow bell pepper, julienned
2 cloves garlic, divided
1/4 cup mayonnaise
1/4 teaspoon crushed red pepper flakes
1/8 teaspoon black pepper
9 ounces artichoke hearts, drained
1 prepared pizza crust, such as Boboli
2 ounces feta cheese, crumbled
1/2 teaspoon dried thyme

Preheat oven to 500 degrees. Heat olive oil in large skillet over medium-high heat. Saute pepper strips 3 minutes. Add 1 clove garlic and saute 1 more minute. Remove from heat. Using a food processor, process remaining clove garlic until smooth; add mayonnaise, red pepper flakes, pepper and artichoke hearts. Process until smooth. Spread sauce on pizza crust and top with cooked peppers. Sprinkle feta cheese and thyme over top. Bake 12 minutes, or until crust is done.

"Delicious! A very nice change from traditional red pizza sauces."
Margo Olsen　　　　　　　**Amador Valley High School, Pleasanton, CA**

BREAKFAST PIZZA

Makes 1 medium pizza

1 tablespoon margarine
1/2 cup potatoes, cooked, diced
1/2 cup sausage, cooked, crumbled
1/2 cup vegetables, diced (onion, red or green bell pepper)
6 large eggs, beaten
1 cup mozzarella cheese, grated
1 green onion, finely chopped
1 (11" or 12") precooked pizza shell, or Boboli crust

Preheat oven to 450 degrees. Place margarine in saute pan over medium heat. Add potatoes, sausage and vegetables; heat thoroughly. Add eggs and scramble lightly. Spread mixture on prepared pizza crust. Top with mozzarella and green onion. Place on pizza stone (if available) and bake 10 to 12 minutes, until cheese is melted.

"I got this recipe from David Will, with the California Egg Commission.
The recipe is used every year at a Pizza Expo held in Las Vegas."
Doris L. Oitzman　　　　　　**Victor Valley High School, Victorville, CA**

CALZONES

Makes 6

1 loaf Bridgford frozen bread
2 cups mozzarella cheese, grated
2 Roma tomatoes, chopped
⅓ cup pizza sauce
1 egg
1 tablespoon water
Optional: Ham, Canadian bacon, green pepper, mushrooms,
    onions, olive, chicken, pesto

Thaw bread and allow to rise. Set oven rack in lowest position. Preheat oven to 450 degrees. Sprinkle baking sheet with cornmeal and set aside. On a lightly floured surface, divide dough into 6 pieces. Cover pieces and let rest while making the filling. Toss together mozzarella cheese, tomato and pizza sauce. Prepare optional ingredients. With a rolling pin, roll each piece of dough into a 6" circle. Spoon about ¼ cup of filling onto half of each circle, leaving a 1" border. Top with optional ingredients. Beat egg and water together with a fork. Moisten edges of the dough with a mixture of egg and water, using pastry brush. Fold the circle in half over the filling. Use the tines of a fork to seal the edges together so none of the filling leaks out as calzone bakes. Transfer calzones to prepared baking sheet. Bake 12 to 15 minutes. Remove from baking sheet and cool on wire rack.

"Time Saving Idea: Many supermarkets have salad bars. You can be creative and have a variety of ingredients with no preparation time (olives, mushrooms, peppers, spinach.) Bag Lunch Idea: Pack each calzone in a small clear plastic bag or freezer bag."

Jan Tuttle   **Mills High School, Millbrae, CA**

EASY ITALIAN PIZZA

Serves 6

1 loaf Bridgford frozen whole wheat bread dough, thawed
½ pound Italian sausage
⅓ cup pizza sauce
1 cup mozzarella cheese, shredded
1 (2 ounce) can mushrooms, sliced, drained
1 (2 ounce) can black olives, sliced, drained
1 green bell pepper, cut into rings
1 red bell pepper, cut into rings
1 yellow bell pepper

Preheat oven to 425 degrees. Press bread dough into lightly greased 12" pizza pan. Cover and let rise about 30 minutes. Bake crust 5 to 7 minutes. Remove from oven. Meanwhile, brown sausage in skillet; drain excess fat, crumble meat and set aside. Spread pizza sauce on crust. Top with mozzarella, sausage, mushrooms and olives. Cut green and red peppers into rings. Use miniature star-shaped cookie cutter to cut yellow peppers into stars. Place peppers on pizza. Bake 15 to 20 minutes or until crust edges are golden brown.

*"This is a very colorful, nutritious and easy pizza.
Very eye-catching with the star-shaped yellow peppers."*

Beth Swift   **La Habra High School, La Habra, CA**

Fire-Roasted Tomato & Garlic Pizza
Serves 4

1 (12") prebaked Italian bread shell
$\frac{1}{2}$ (26 ounce) jar Classico di Siena
(Fire Roasted Tomato & Garlic) Pasta Sauce
1 $\frac{1}{2}$ cups mozzarella cheese, shredded
1 (6 ounce) package Italian Style fully cooked chicken breast strips
$\frac{1}{2}$ (small) yellow squash, sliced
$\frac{1}{2}$ (small) zucchini, sliced
1 (2 $\frac{1}{4}$ ounce) can ripe olives, sliced, drained

Preheat oven to 400 degrees. Place bread shell on baking sheet. Top with pasta sauce. Sprinkle with cheese; top with chicken and vegetables. Bake 15 minutes or until hot and cheese is melted. Let stand 5 minutes before serving.

Borden Foods Corporation   **Columbus, OH**

Goat Cheese Pizza with Capicola
Serves 4

1 pound pizza dough, room temperature OR 1 prepared pizza crust
1 (28 ounce) can Italian peeled tomatoes, patted dry
2 tablespoons olive oil
1 teaspoon garlic, minced
$\frac{1}{2}$ teaspoon dried oregano, crumbled
$\frac{1}{4}$ teaspoon crushed red pepper
5 ounces mild goat cheese, shredded
2 ounces capicola, thinly sliced

Preheat oven to 500 degrees. Preheat a pizza stone or oil a large baking sheet. In a large bowl, combine tomatoes with olive oil, garlic, oregano and red pepper; let stand 15 minutes. Roll out dough on lightly floured surface. Top with tomatoes, goat cheese and capicola. Bake 10 min. on stone or about 16 min. on baking sheet.

Jan Schulenburg   **Irvine High School, Irvine, CA**

Julie's Pizza
Makes 1 medium pizza

1 package rapid rise yeast
$\frac{3}{4}$ cup very warm water (105 to 115 degrees)
2 cups flour
$\frac{1}{2}$ teaspoon salt
1 teaspoon olive oil
1 tablespoon cornmeal
$\frac{1}{2}$ cup (4 ounces) tomato sauce
3 ounces tomato paste
1 teaspoon sugar
$\frac{1}{2}$ teaspoon dried oregano
1 clove garlic, minced
1 cup cheese, shredded
$\frac{1}{2}$ pound cooked sausage, cooked ground beef or 12 slices pepperoni

Preheat oven to 425 degrees. Dissolve yeast in warm water. Blend flour and salt into yeast mixture to form dough. Turn dough onto lightly floured surface; knead 5 minutes. Cover and let rest 5 minutes. Brush pizza pan with olive oil, sprinkle with corn meal. Roll out dough into 13" circle. Place in pizza pan with 1" of dough overlapping the edge, shaping a ½" rim at edge of pan. Mix tomato sauce, tomato paste, sugar and spices together in a small mixing bowl. Spread on pizza crust. Top with cheese and desired toppings. Bake about 15 to 20 minutes, until crust is golden.

"If freshmen can do it, so can you!"

Julie Carriere　　　　　**No. Monterey Co. High School, Castroville, CA**

MARGHERITE PIZZA

Serves 2 - 4　　　　　　　　　　　　*Photo opposite page 96*

　1 pre-baked (12") pizza crust
　3 (medium) Roma tomatoes, sliced ⅛" thick
　8 ounces Wisconsin Fresh Mozzarella cheese, sliced ⅛" thick
　12 to 14 leaves fresh basil, julienned
　¼ cup pine nuts
　1 tablespoon garlic olive oil, optional

Arrange tomato slices on crust. Arrange fresh mozzarella slices on tomatoes. Sprinkle fresh basil over cheese. Sprinkle pine nuts over top. Drizzle garlic oil over top, if desired. Bake at 450 degrees for 7 to 9 minutes or until crust is lightly browned and cheese is melted.

Wisconsin Milk Marketing Board, Inc.　　　　　　　**Madison, WI**

MESQUITE CHICKEN PIZZA

Serves 4

　1 (10 ounce) can Pillsbury Pizza Crust
　2 Tyson's Mesquite chicken breasts, chopped
　8 ounces mozzarella cheese, shredded
　4 ounces Provolone cheese, shredded
　¼ cup Parmesan cheese, grated
　4 ounces hickory smoke flavored barbecue sauce
　⅛ red onion, thinly sliced into 1" strips
　½ cup black olives, sliced
　½ cup mushrooms, sliced
　2 to 3 tablespoons cilantro, freshly chopped

Preheat oven to 425 degrees. Lightly grease 12" pizza pan. Unroll dough, plan on pan and start putting into place, working from center out, with fingers. Bake 7 minutes or until crust just begins to brown. Meanwhile, cook chicken breasts according to package directions, then cut into bite-size pieces when cooled. In a large bowl, mix the three cheeses and set aside. Spread barbecue sauce on partially baked pizza crust and top with cheeses. Layer chicken, onion, olives and mushrooms on top. Sprinkle cilantro over all and bake 10 to 15 minutes or until crust is golden brown and cheeses are melted.

Variation: Eliminate barbecue sauce and use a cheese sauce, cheese, thinly sliced zucchini, red onion, ground chicken and lemon pepper seasoning - another culinary delight!

"This is a combination of all our family's favorites and is preferred over traditional pizza. My Foods I classes and Gourmet class NEVER have leftovers on this one!"

Toni Carnes　　　　　　　　**Exeter High School, Exeter, CA**

PEPPERONI PIZZA PIE
Serves 8

1 (10 ounce) can Pillsbury refrigerated All Ready Pizza Crust
4 ounces (1 cup) mozzarella cheese, shredded
1 (2 ounce) package pepperoni, sliced
1 (2.5 ounce) jar mushrooms, sliced, drained
1/2 cup prepared pizza sauce
1 tablespoon Parmesan cheese, grated

Heat oven to 425 degrees. Grease 9" round pan. Unroll dough and place in prepared pan with corners of dough extending over edges of pan. Lightly press dough into pan. Sprinkle mozzarella cheese over bottom of dough. Top with pepperoni, mushrooms and sauce. Bring corners of dough to center, pine-wheel fashion; twist ends of dough together. Sprinkle with Parmesan cheese. Bake 15 to 20 minutes until golden brown. Serve immediately.

"This recipe is well liked by my students in Foods classes.
It's easy to make in one class period of time."
Joyce Grohmann   **Los Amigos High School, Garden Grove, CA**

PESTO CHICKEN PIZZA
Serves 4 - 6

1 (12") pre-baked pizza crust
7 ounces pesto with basil, prepared
1 (14.5 ounce) Del Monte diced tomatoes with basil, garlic & oregano
2 1/2 pounds chicken breast, boneless, cooked
2 cups mozzarella cheese, shredded
1/2 cup mild cheddar cheese, shredded
1 small red pepper, thinly sliced
1/2 to 1 (small) zucchini, thinly sliced
4 to 5 (medium) mushrooms, sliced
1 (2.5 ounce) can olives, sliced
Garnish: Parmesan cheese, grated, fresh basil (optional)

Preheat oven to 450 degrees. Place crust on baking sheet. Spread pesto evenly over crust. Place tomatoes and chicken over pesto. Top with mozzarella and cheddar cheese. Add red pepper, zucchini, mushrooms and olives. Bake 10 minutes or until hot and bubbly. Garnish with Parmesan and fresh basil.

"Have a little green leaf lettuce, carrots and Italian dressing on the side
and this makes a wonderful meal that all of my family loves."
Betty Byrne   **Vaca Pena Middle School, Vacaville, CA**

Toppings stay on pizza much better when cheese
is on the bottom rather than on the top.

Toni Carnes   **Exeter HS, Exeter, CA**

PIZZA
Serves 6

Dough:
1/2 package yeast
1/2 cup + 2 tablespoons warm water
1 tablespoon cooking or olive oil
1/2 teaspoon salt
1 3/4 cup flour
Sauce:
1 (8 ounce) can tomato sauce
1/2 teaspoon oregano
1/4 teaspoon salt
1/4 teaspoon pepper
1/4 teaspoon rosemary
1/4 teaspoon thyme
Toppings:
1 cup mozzarella cheese, grated
1/2 pound sausage or ground beef, cooked
1 link pepperoni, sliced
1/3 cup mushrooms, olives, green pepper or onion, chopped
2 tablespoons Parmesan cheese, grated

Dough: Dissolve yeast in water. Add oil and salt. Blend in flour to make a stiff dough. Knead lightly on floured surface. Place in greased bowl, turn to grease top. Cover and let rise until doubled.

Sauce: Combine all sauce ingredients together and stir.

Toppings: Prepare as desired.

Assembly: Preheat oven to 450 degrees. Roll dough into 14" circle. Place on pizza pan or cookie sheet. Roll edges to make stand-up ridge. Cover dough with sauce and sprinkle with cheese. Top with desired toppings. Bake 25 to 30 minutes.

"The olive oil gives a much better flavor to the crust.
Can also use pre-made crust or dough."

Donna Lile   **Western High School, Las Vegas, NV**

PIZZA PIE
Serves 6

1 cup Bisquick
1/4 cup butter
2 tablespoons boiling water
1 pound turkey sausage
1 onion, minced
1 pound cottage cheese
3 eggs, beaten
1/4 cup Parmesan cheese, grated
1/4 teaspoon pepper
1/3 cup parsley
1/2 pound mozzarella cheese, shredded

Preheat oven to 375 degrees. Combine Bisquick, butter and boiling water; press into 10" deep pie pan. Prick well with fork. Bake 10 minutes; remove and set aside.

Brown turkey sausage and onion until crumbly and pink color has disappeared; drain fat. Mix cottage cheese, eggs, Parmesan cheese, pepper and parsley. Turn into baked crust. Top with mozzarella cheese. Bake 25 minutes or until knife inserted in center comes out clean.

"This was a recipe prepared frequently by one of my college roommates many years ago."
DeLisa Davis   **Sutter High School, Sutter, CA**

PIZZA PLANKS
Serves 6

- 1 loaf French bread
- 12 ounce jar spaghetti sauce
- 12 ounces mozzarella cheese, grated
- 4 ounces pepperoni slices

Split bread in half lengthwise. Cut each half into 3 equal pieces. Remove some of the soft bread to make a slightly hollowed loaf. Spoon spaghetti sauce evenly over all pieces. Sprinkle with cheese. Arrange pepperoni slices oven on top. Microwave each pizza for 1 ½ minutes on HIGH. Rotate plate ¼ turn. Microwave on HIGH 1 ½ minutes more, until cheese is melted.

Linda Stroup   **Virgin Valley High School, Mesquite, NV**

QUICK TORTILLA PIZZAS
Serves 10

- 1 (15 ounce) can tomato sauce
- 1 tablespoon Italian seasoning
- ½ to 1 teaspoon garlic powder
- ½ teaspoon sugar
- 1 to 2 tablespoons olive oil
- 1 package flour tortillas (large, 10 to a package)
- 2 to 3 cups mozzarella cheese, grated
- ½ cup Parmesan cheese, grated
- *Assorted Toppings:* (as desired) Pepperoni, sausage,
  bell pepper, onion, olives

Place first 5 ingredients in a medium saucepan. Simmer 10 to 15 minutes. Line a baking sheet with 3 to 4 tortillas. Spread heated sauce on tortillas, sprinkle with cheeses and add desired toppings, Bake 10 to 12 minutes, until heated through and bubbly. Repeat with remaining ingredients.

" You can also use English muffins, hamburger buns, corn tortillas,
French rolls - anything for the bread. Bottled marinara sauce is fine also."
Carla Escola   **Sierra High School, Manteca, CA**

RUNNER'S PIZZA

Serves 4

Sauce:
1 cup tomato sauce
2 tablespoons onion, chopped
1 clove garlic, minced
$\frac{1}{2}$ teaspoon oregano
$\frac{1}{2}$ teaspoon basil
dash salt and pepper
Crust & Toppings:
$\frac{3}{4}$ cup spiral pasta
1 package yeast
1 cup warm water (105 to 115 degrees)
1 $\frac{3}{4}$ cup all-purpose flour
$\frac{1}{2}$ cup whole wheat flour
$\frac{1}{4}$ cup rolled oats
2 tablespoons olive oil
nonstick cooking spray
cornmeal
3 cups lowfat mozzarella cheese, shredded
$\frac{1}{4}$ cup Parmesan cheese, grated

Sauce: Combine all sauce ingredients and simmer until onions are tender.
Crust: Cook pasta according to package direction; drain and set aside. Dissolve yeast in warm water. Stir in flour, whole wheat flour, oats and oil. Turn onto lightly floured surface and knead until smooth and elastic, about 20 times. Cover and let rest 20 minutes. Preheat oven to 400 degrees. Roll dough into a 14" round. Put on pan that has been lightly greased with nonstick cooking spray and sprinkled with cornmeal. Top with half of the sauce, pasta, remaining sauce and cheeses. Bake 20 to 25 minutes.

Dale Sheehan   **Santana High School, Santee, CA**

SEARED AHI TUNA PIZZA

Makes 1 pizza

1 precooked pizza crust
Artichoke spread:
$\frac{1}{3}$ cup marinated artichoke hearts, drained, chopped
1 to 2 tablespoons canned, sweet red peppers, minced
1 teaspoon garlic, minced
1 tablespoon lemon juice
3 tablespoons mayonnaise
1 fresh Ahi tuna fillet, cooked rare, thinly sliced
4 to 6 mushrooms, fresh or canned, thinly sliced
1 cup Cojita cheese, crumbled or mild goat or feta cheese
several pinches dill weed
$\frac{1}{4}$ cup Parmesan cheese, freshly grated

Preheat oven to 375 degrees. Place crust on pizza pan. Combine artichokes, sweet red peppers, garlic, lemon juice and mayonnaise. Cover pizza crust with thin layer of artichoke spread. Layer with remaining ingredients and bake at 375 degrees until heated through.

Sandra Massey   **Mt. View High School, El Monte, CA**

STUFFED CRUST PEPPERONI PIZZA
Makes 1 pizza

1 (10 ounce) Pillsbury Pizza Crust
6 pieces string cheese
$\frac{1}{2}$ cup prepared pizza sauce
pepperoni slices, as desired
8 ounces mozzarella cheese, grated

Preheat oven to 425 degrees. Grease or spray a 9" x 13" pan. Unroll pizza dough and press in bottom and 1" up sides of pan. Place pieces of string cheese along inside edge of dough. Fold 1" of dough over and around cheese; press dough edges to seal. Top crust with sauce, pepperoni and mozzarella cheese. Bake 15 to 28 minutes or until crust is golden brown and cheese is melted.

Diane Wolak   Martin Luther King High School, Riverside, CA

THE BEST HOMEMADE PIZZA
Serves 4

Dough:
2 $\frac{1}{4}$ cups flour
1 package dry yeast
$\frac{3}{4}$ teaspoon salt
$\frac{1}{2}$ teaspoon sugar
$\frac{3}{4}$ cup hot water
nonstick cooking spray
Sauce:
1 cup tomato sauce
1 teaspoon oregano
1 clove garlic
Toppings:
1 cup mozzarella cheese, shredded
1 cup pepperoni, sliced, or cooked and crumbled Italian sausage
assorted sliced vegetables

Dough: Using a food processor, mix flour, yeast, salt and sugar. With processor running, slowly add water. Process until dough forms a ball. Process 1 minute longer, until dough is smooth and elastic. Remove from food processor and place on floured surface. Cover with plastic wrap and let rest 10 minutes. Grease a pizza pan with nonstick cooking spray. Roll out dough to fit pan. Move oven rack to lowest shelf and preheat oven to 500 degrees.

Sauce: Mix sauce ingredients together and spread on dough.

Toppings: Sprinkle with cheese and desired toppings. Bake 10 to 15 minutes.

"After years of searching for a great pizza recipe, this one has been very popular in our classes. The dough can be made ahead and refrigerated up to a week! Don't let the yeast scare you. I use this with my beginning cooking students. It comes out just like pizzaria pizza. Begin dough the night before for an easy, quick dinner."

Debbie Harvey   Amador Valley High School, Pleasanton, CA
Beth Gonzales   Bolsa Grande High School, Garden Grove, CA

Main Dishes
Chicken & Turkey

A DIFFERENT CHICKEN PARMESAN
Serves 6 - 7

    5 to 7 boneless, skinless chicken breasts
    1 pint whipping cream
    1 $\frac{1}{2}$ cups Parmesan cheese, freshly grated
    3 cups noodles, hot, cooked

Place chicken breasts in a 9" x 13" glass dish. Cover with whipping cream. Sprinkle with grated Parmesan and cover with foil. Bake at 350 degrees 30 minutes. Remove foil and continue baking 15 minutes, until chicken is completely cooked. Serve over hot, cooked noodles.

"This is a different kind of chicken Parmesan."

Karen Frey   **Hesperia High School, Hesperia, CA**

AUTHENTIC ITALIAN CHICKEN PARMESAN
Serves 6

    Tomato Sauce:
    2 tablespoons olive oil
    1 (large) onion, very finely chopped
    6 cloves garlic, minced
    1 (28 ounce) can whole peeled tomatoes with thick tomato puree
    1 $\frac{1}{2}$ teaspoons dried basil
    1 cup red wine
    1 $\frac{1}{2}$ teaspoons dried oregano
    $\frac{1}{2}$ teaspoon salt
    $\frac{1}{2}$ teaspoon pepper
    Chicken:
    6 boneless, skinless chicken breast halves
    1 $\frac{1}{2}$ cups Parmesan cheese, freshly grated, divided
    1 cup Italian dry bread crumbs
    2 teaspoons dried oregano
    1 cup all-purpose flour
    2 eggs
    2 tablespoons butter
    2 tablespoons olive oil
    8 ounces mozzarella cheese, shredded
    6 ounces spaghetti
    $\frac{1}{2}$ cup fresh parsley, minced

Sauce: In a deep skillet, heat olive oil over medium high heat; add onion and garlic and cook until very soft, about 10 minutes. Stir in tomatoes with puree, basil, wine, oregano and salt and pepper. Break up tomatoes with spoon. Bring to a simmer, then reduce heat to low and simmer until mixture thickens, about 30 minutes. Transfer sauce to large measuring cup or bowl and set aside. Wipe skillet clean and set side.

Chicken: Preheat oven to 375 degrees. On work surface, wrap 3 pieces chicken in plastic wrap. Pound out breasts with meat mallet to about ¼" thickness. Repeat with remaining breasts. In a shallow bowl, mix 1 cup Parmesan cheese with bread crumbs, oregano and salt. Place flour and eggs in separate bowls. Beat eggs. Coat each chicken piece with flour, dip into eggs. Coat with Parmesan mixture. Place on ungreased baking sheet. In same skillet used to make sauce, melt butter and oil over medium-high heat. Add chicken, in batches, and cook, turning once, until golden brown, 2 to 3 minutes each side. Place all chicken in a 9" x 13" baking dish, overlapping pieces. Pour all sauce over chicken, except for ½ cup. Sprinkle mozzarella and remaining Parmesan cheese over top. Bake until cheese is golden, about 15 to 18 minutes. Cook pasta according to package directions. Drain pasta and return to pot. Toss with remaining ½ cup sauce. Place chicken on warm pasta and sprinkle with parsley.

"I'm of Italian descent. My family was born in a little Italy, New York neighborhood. We grew up on old fashion food, owned and operated an old-fashion deli/market called Old World Deli. I was one of the licensed caterers. I was also attending college as a food science teacher in hopes of producing educated young entrepreneurs of the future. I would like to be instrumental in bringing authentic Italian cooking to your home!"

Laura Zerpoli   **Monrovia High School, Monrovia, CA**

CARTWHEELS WITH SAUSAGE
Serves 4

1 teaspoon garlic, chopped
1 to 2 teaspoons olive oil
½ pound turkey sausage
¼ pound mushrooms, sliced
1 ¼ cups canned Italian plum tomatoes,
    with their juice, coarsely chopped
½ cup whole milk or cream
salt and pepper, to taste
1 pound pasta cartwheels
Garnish: Parmesan cheese, freshly grated

Put garlic and olive oil in a skillet and turn heat to medium. When garlic becomes pale gold in color, add sausage. After sausage turns brown, add mushrooms and cook until mushrooms are tender. Add tomatoes and gently simmer about 10 minutes. Add milk or cream and turn up heat. Cook 1 to 2 minutes, stirring frequently, until milk is reduced. Add salt and pepper to taste. Remove from heat. Drop pasta into large pot of boiling, salted water. When it is barely tender, but firm to the bite, drain and toss immediately with sauce. Serve at once with freshly grated Parmesan cheese.

"This is a recipe I've adapted from Marcella Hazan."

Julie Blanchard   **Western High School, Anaheim, CA**

Chicken Amaretto
Serves 6 - 8

1 teaspoon salt
$\frac{1}{2}$ teaspoon pepper
$\frac{1}{4}$ teaspoon garlic powder
$\frac{1}{4}$ teaspoon curry powder
$\frac{1}{4}$ cup flour
$\frac{1}{4}$ cup butter
8 chicken breast halves, boneless, skinless, cut into 1" strips
$\frac{1}{2}$ pound fresh mushrooms, sliced
$\frac{1}{4}$ cup Amaretto liqueur
juice of 1 lemon
rind of 1 lemon, grated
1 tablespoon cornstarch
2 tablespoons water
1 $\frac{1}{2}$ cups chicken broth

Mix together, in a plastic bag, salt, pepper, garlic powder, curry powder and flour. Melt butter in large skillet over medium-high heat. Shake chicken pieces in bag and saute quickly in butter; reduce heat to medium-low. Add mushrooms, Amaretto, lemon juice and rind; simmer 5 minutes. In a small bowl, combine cornstarch with water to form paste; blend into chicken broth. Stir mixture into skillet with chicken; cook over low heat, stirring constantly until mixture bubbles and thickens.

"This recipe is a delicious change for chicken breasts. Everyone loves this entree and it's quick to prepare!"

Barbara Adams   **Merced High School, Merced, CA**

Chicken & Sun-Dried Tomato Crust
Serves 4

2 cups seasoned bread crumbs
$\frac{1}{2}$ cup sun dried tomatoes, oil packed, drained and reserved
3 $\frac{1}{2}$ tablespoons oil, reserved from tomatoes, divided
2 cloves garlic
4 chicken breast halves, with skin and bones
salt and pepper, to taste

Combine bread crumbs, tomatoes and 2 tablespoons oil along with garlic in food processor. Pulse until tomatoes are coarsely chopped. Preheat oven to 375 degrees. Season chicken with salt and pepper. Heat remaining oil in large skillet. Add chicken, skin side down and cook until skin is crisp and golden, about 5 minutes. Transfer chicken, skin side up to baking sheet. Top with bread crumb mixture, pressing to adhere. Bake until chicken is cooked through, about 30 minutes.

"The topping can be made ahead and refrigerated for a quick preparation in the evening. This is a wonderfully flavorful dish."

Delaine Smith   **West Valley High School, Cottonwood, CA**

CHICKEN CACCIATORE
Serves 8

6 tablespoons salad oil
5 to 6 pounds chicken pieces
1 cup onion, minced
$3/4$ cup green pepper, minced
4 cloves garlic, minced
1 (1 pound, 13 ounce) can tomatoes
1 (8 ounce) can tomato sauce
$1/2$ cup chianti wine
3 $3/4$ teaspoons salt
$1/2$ teaspoon pepper
$1/2$ teaspoon allspice
2 bay leaves
$1/2$ teaspoon dried thyme
dash cayenne pepper

Heat oil over medium-high heat. Saute chicken until golden on all sides. Add onions, green pepper and garlic; brown lightly. Add remaining ingredients and simmer, uncovered, 30 to 40 minutes, or until chicken is fork tender. Serve over hot, cooked rice.

*"This recipe is a family favorite served over rice.
You may use skinless chicken if you're watching your fat grams."*

Jeanette Yee **Capuchino High School, San Bruno, CA**

CHICKEN ITALIANA
Serves 6

2 $1/2$ pounds chicken pieces
1 teaspoon salt
$1/4$ teaspoon pepper
1 tablespoon vegetable oil
1 pound sweet Italian sausage, cut into bite-sized pieces
1 teaspoon garlic, minced
$1/2$ cup chicken broth
1 cup onion, chopped
1 green pepper, cut into 1" squares
1 teaspoon oregano
1 teaspoon basil
1 teaspoon sugar

Sprinkle chicken with salt and pepper. Heat vegetable oil in large skillet. Brown chicken; remove and set aside. Brown sausage and drain on paper towel. Pour off excess fat from skillet and add all remaining ingredients; mix well. Arrange browned chicken and sausage over contents in skillet. Cover and simmer 30 to 40 minutes or until chicken is tender.

"After assembling this dish, it may be refrigerated for up to a day before final cooking. This dish is great served with a pasta and sprinkled with freshly grated Parmesan cheese."

Linda Paskins **Cordova High School, Rancho Cordova, CA**

CHICKEN MARINARA
Serves 4

nonstick cooking spray
4 boneless chicken breast halves (about 1 pound)
2 cups fresh mushrooms, sliced
3 cloves garlic, minced
1 teaspoon dried basil
$\frac{1}{2}$ teaspoon Italian seasoning
1 (28 ounce) jar meatless spaghetti sauce
$\frac{1}{2}$ cup red wine or chicken broth
angel hair pasta or spaghetti, hot, cooked

In a nonstick skillet coated with nonstick cooking spray, cook chicken for 6 minutes on each side; remove from pan and keep warm. Add mushrooms, garlic, basil and Italian seasoning to skillet. Saute until mushrooms are tender. Stir in spaghetti sauce and wine or broth. Add chicken; cover and simmer 10 minutes or until heated through. Serve over hot, cooked pasta.

"This skillet recipe can be prepared in minutes.
Add an Italian bread and salad to complete the meal."

Donna Baker　　　　　**Redlands East Valley High School, Redlands, CA**

CHICKEN MARSALA
Serves 4 - 6

4 to 6 chicken breasts, boned, skinned
3 tablespoons flour
$\frac{1}{2}$ teaspoon salt
$\frac{1}{4}$ teaspoon pepper
2 tablespoons extra virgin olive oil
2 teaspoons margarine
$\frac{1}{4}$ cup marsala wine (Italian cooking sherry)
2 tablespoons chicken broth
2 tablespoons lemon juice
$\frac{1}{2}$ cup mushrooms, sliced (optional)
1 thin slice prosciutto, (optional)
1 thin slice mozzarella cheese (optional)

Pound chicken fillets flat with a meat hammer. Dust the breasts lightly with flour, salt and pepper. Line the bottom of a thick frying pan with olive oil and margarine. Quickly cook one side of the dusted breasts, 2 to 3 minutes. Turn over, lower heat and pour marsala wine, chicken broth and lemon juice over chicken. Add mushrooms, if using. Cover pan with a lid and simmer about 15 to 20 minutes. At the last minute, add a slice of prosciutto and mozzarella cheese, if using. Turn off heat, replace lid and let melt. Serve with as much of the glazed sauce and mushrooms you can smother on! Bon Apetit!

"Peggy Keller is proud of her Italian heritage and generously
shared one of her quick favorites with us."

Judith Huffman　　　　　**Mariposa High School, Mariposa, CA**

CHICKEN PICASSO

Serves 4

2 tablespoons butter
½ cup flour
3 to 4 boneless, skinless chicken breasts or tenders
2 tablespoons cornstarch
¼ cup Triple Sec or brandy
4 cups fresh fruit, cut up (melons and pineapple give nice flavor)
1 clove garlic, chopped
1 onion, chopped
salt and pepper, to taste

Melt butter in saute pan or wok. Flour chicken and brown in melted butter. Remove to serving platter and keep warm. Stir cornstarch into Triple Sec or brandy until smooth and dissolved; pour into saute pan and add fruit, garlic, onion and seasonings. Stir over low heat until fruit is heated and sauce is thickened. Pour sauce over chicken and serve. NOTE: This is especially good served with rice pilaf or wild rice.

"This recipe was given to me by one of our sons, Jeremy, who has worked for several fine-dining restaurants. This was a dish that he particularly likes himself and wanted to be able to make it at home. It's a hit!"

Linda Heinbach　　　　　　　　**Yosemite High School, Oakhurst, CA**

CHICKEN SALTIMBOCCA

Serves 6 - 8

6 whole boneless, skinless chicken breasts, halved
1 cup + 1 tablespoon flour, divided
⅓ cup butter, melted
12 thin slices prosciutto ham
6 slices provolone cheese
¼ cup shallots, chopped
3 cloves garlic, minced
½ pound mushrooms, sliced
½ cup dry white wine
1 cup chicken broth
½ teaspoon dried thyme
½ teaspoon dried oregano
½ cup dry sherry
½ cup cream
salt and pepper, to taste

Lightly coat chicken in 1 cup flour. Melt butter in skillet and brown chicken. Arrange in a 13" x 9" baking dish. Top each breast with prosciutto and ½ slice cheese. In same skillet, saute shallots and garlic until soft. Add mushrooms, white wine, broth and herbs. Bring to a boil and cook 10 minutes. In a separate dish, blend 1 tablespoon flour and a small amount of sherry. Pour into hot sauce. Stir in remaining sherry and cream. Season with salt and pepper. Pour over chicken and bake at 375 degrees for 30 minutes.

"This easy dish is elegant enough for company and veal can be substituted for chicken."
Angela Croce　　　　　　　　**Mira Mesa High School, San Diego, CA**

CHICKEN ZUCCHINI LASAGNA

Serves 9 - 12

9 lasagna noodles, uncooked
3 boneless, skinless chicken breasts
garlic salt, to taste
pepper, to taste
2 (small) zucchini
2 cans cream of chicken soup
8 ounces sour cream
8 ounces Parmesan cheese, grated
$\frac{1}{4}$ cup skim milk
1 teaspoon Italian seasoning
$\frac{1}{8}$ teaspoon garlic powder
1 cup cheddar cheese, shredded

Prepare noodles as directed on package; set aside. Split whole chicken breasts and season with garlic salt and pepper, to taste. Boil in water for 30 minutes. Cool and cut into bite size pieces; set aside. Grate or thinly slice zucchini and set aside. In a saucepan over low heat, mix together soup, sour cream, Parmesan cheese, milk, Italian seasoning and garlic powder. Butter bottom of a 9" x 13" casserole dish and spread with a little of the white sauce. Layer ingredients, beginning with noodles, sauce, chicken, zucchini; repeat, ending with sauce. Sprinkle with cheddar cheese. Bake at 350 degrees for 45 minutes and serve.

"This recipe is shared by my daughter, Danielle Winter.
She sold these books when she was in 8th grade and now she is in one! She loves to cook!"
Betty Bundy   **Hidden Valley Middle School, Escondido, CA**

CLASSIC CHICKEN PARMESAN

Serves 6

6 boneless, skinless chicken breasts, pounded thin
2 eggs, lightly beaten
1 cup Italian seasoned bread crumbs
2 tablespoons olive oil
1 (26 ounce) jar spaghetti sauce
1 cup mozzarella cheese, shredded

Dip chicken breasts in eggs, then in bread crumbs, coating well. Heat olive oil in large skillet and brown chicken; drain on paper towels. In 9" x 13" baking dish, spread 1 cup spaghetti sauce. Arrange chicken in dish, then top with remaining sauce. Sprinkle with shredded cheese and bake at 375 degrees for 25 minutes.

"Easy. Serve with a green salad and garlic bread for a very quick meal."
Adriana Molinaro   **Granite Hills High School, El Cajon, CA**

EASY CHEESY PARMESAN CHICKEN STRIPS

Serves 4

$\frac{1}{3}$ cup seasoned bread crumbs
$\frac{2}{3}$ cup Parmesan cheese (or Parmesan/Romano blend), grated
1 teaspoon Italian seasoning
2 tablespoons butter or margarine, melted
2 tablespoons olive oil
2 whole boneless, skinless chicken breasts, cut into 1" strips

Mushroom Frittata
Great for breakfast or anytime.
(page 119)

Beef & Spinach Lasagna
Noodles cook while baking.
(page 85)

Preheat oven to 350 degrees. Mix bread crumbs, cheese and Italian seasoning in a flat pan. Mix melted butter or margarine and olive oil in another flat pan. Coat chicken strips in oil/butter mixture and roll in breading mix. Lay strips in a flat baking dish and cook 40 to 45 minutes. NOTE: You can also use this recipe for zucchini strips; cook right along with chicken strips or all by themselves using the batter recipe above.

"These are delicious and are wonderful for those watching their carbohydrate intake."
Val Herford   **Mesa Intermediate School, Palmdale, CA**

EASY CROCK POT CHICKEN CACCIATORE
Serves 4

1 (2.5 to 3 pound) chicken, cut up
$\frac{1}{4}$ cup olive oil
1 onion, sliced
2 (6 ounce) cans tomato paste
1 (4 ounce) can mushrooms
1 teaspoon salt
$\frac{1}{2}$ teaspoon pepper
1 to 2 cloves garlic, minced
1 to 2 teaspoons oregano leaves
$\frac{1}{2}$ teaspoon basil
1 bay leaf
$\frac{1}{4}$ to $\frac{1}{2}$ cup dry red wine
1 pound cooked spaghetti
1 tablespoon butter
Garnish: Parmesan cheese, grated

In a skillet, brown chicken in hot oil. Place chicken in the crockpot. Combine all other ingredients, except spaghetti and butter in a bowl and pour over chicken. Cover and cook on low 7 to 9 hours. Prepare spaghetti according to package directions; drain and toss with butter. Serve chicken over hot, buttered spaghetti. Serve with grated Parmesan cheese.

"You can substitute Herbes de Provence for the herbs."
Bonnie Shrock   **Kearny High School, San Diego, CA**

FETTUCCINI CHICKEN & MUSHROOMS
Serves 4

4 tablespoons butter
1 boneless, skinless chicken breast,
    (about 8 ounces) cut into $\frac{3}{4}$" pieces
12 ounces mushrooms (use a mixture of white,
    button, shitake and oyster)
$\frac{1}{2}$ cup scallions, thinly sliced
1 clove garlic, minced
$\frac{1}{2}$ cup heavy cream
1 (14.5 ounce) can whole peeled tomatoes, drained, chopped
1 cup frozen baby peas
$\frac{1}{2}$ teaspoon salt
freshly ground pepper, to taste
12 ounces fresh or 8 ounces dry fettuccini
2 tablespoons fresh parsley, chopped
Parmesan cheese, grated

Heat butter in large, heavy skillet. Add chicken and saute until edges are golden, about 5 minutes. Cut mushrooms into $1/8$" to $1/4$" slices. Discard tough stems from shitake mushrooms. Add to chicken and saute until tender, about 5 minutes. Add scallions and garlic; saute 2 minutes. Add heavy cream and tomatoes; heat until boiling over medium-high heat; reduce heat to low and simmer until sauce is thickened. Add the peas, salt and pepper. Heat, stirring until peas are tender. Meanwhile, cook fettuccini in plenty of boiling, salted water until al dente; 2 minutes for fresh or 5 to 7 minutes for dried; drain. Place fettuccini in a large serving bowl. Top with chicken and mushrooms and toss. Sprinkle with parsley and Parmesan cheese.

"Hannah, a student in 1995, gave me this wonderful book entitled 365 Ways To Cook Pasta. *This is one of the many delicious recipes in this book. Thank you again, Hannah!"*
Darlene V. Brown   Golden Valley Middle School, San Bernardino, CA

GRANDMA JO'S CHICKEN PARMESAN
Serves 8

1 clove garlic, minced
$1/4$ onion, chopped
few sprigs parsley, chopped
$1/2$ to 1 cup olive oil (as needed for sauteing), divided
1 (28 ounce) can crushed tomatoes, blended
$1/2$ cup water
1 tablespoon sugar
8 chicken breasts
1 egg, beaten
$1/3$ cup Parmesan cheese
1 cup Italian bread crumbs
1 cup mozzarella cheese, grated

Saute garlic, onion and parsley in small amount of oil until onion is soft; remove from pan. In another saucepan, add onion/garlic mixture along with tomatoes, water and sugar and simmer, uncovered, 45 minutes. Meanwhile, dip chicken in egg, then in Italian bread crumbs that have been combined with Parmesan cheese. Fry in small amount of oil until lightly browned on each side. Pat excess oil with paper towels and place chicken in oblong baking pan on a small amount of sauce. Lightly cover chicken with tomato sauce and sprinkle with mozzarella. Bake at 350 degrees 30 to 40 minutes. NOTE: I like to cut some of the chicken breasts in half before breading - better size for kids. Also, you can double the recipe for the sauce and serve with pasta.

"When time is limited, Prego sauce works great. This is a favorite of mine, from my Italian grandmother. When she comes to visit, we sure enjoy her wonderful recipes!"
Janine Walton   Etiwanda High School, Etiwanda, CA

Don't' use a colander to drain long flat pasta, like fettuccini. Let the excess water drip back into the pot, then add strands to the sauce. This enables the pasta's starch to add body to the sauce.

Judy Dobkins   Redlands HS, Redlands, CA

Green Chicken Lasagna
Serves 12

- 2 chicken breasts
- 1 pint ricotta cheese
- 1 egg
- 2 cups mozzarella cheese, divided
- 1 teaspoon garlic salt
- 1 cup green enchilada sauce
- 9 lasagna noodles

Boil chicken and dice. Mix ricotta cheese, egg, 1 ½ cups mozzarella, chicken and garlic salt. Cover bottom of 9" x 13" pan with enchilada sauce. Place 3 lasagna noodles in pan. Cover with ½ cheese mixture. Repeat layering 2 more times. Sprinkle remaining ½ cup mozzarella cheese on top. Cover and bake at 350 degrees for 30 minutes. Remove foil and bake 15 minutes more.

Katrina Brighton   **Swainston Middle School, N. Las Vegas, NV**

Italian Chicken
Serves 4

- 4 boneless, skinless chicken breast halves
- 1 ½ cups Italian dressing
- 1 ½ cups Italian bread crumbs

Marinate chicken in dressing at least 1 hour or overnight. Roll marinated chicken in bread crumbs and bake at 350 degrees for 30 minutes, or until done. (Cooking time varies with the size of chicken breasts.)

*"This recipe can be adapted to feed 2 or 10. It's one of the first meals
I learned to cook, and it's always a big hit!"*

Jill Perry   **Mojave High School, N. Las Vegas, NV**

Italian Chicken with Artichokes
Serves 8

- 2 (6 ounce) jars marinated artichoke hearts
- 4 tablespoons olive oil
- ¼ cup flour
- 8 boneless skinless chicken breast halves
- 6 tomatoes, peeled and quartered OR 1 (16 ounce) can tomatoes
- 4 small cloves garlic, minced
- 1 pound fresh mushrooms, trimmed, sliced
- 1 cup dry sherry
- 2 tablespoons fresh parsley, minced
- 1 ½ teaspoons salt
- ¾ teaspoon pepper
- 1 teaspoon dried oregano
- 1 teaspoon dried basil

Drain artichokes, reserving marinade. Combine ½ of the marinade with olive oil in a 10" to 12" skillet; heat over medium-high heat. Place flour in a paper bag. Coat chicken breasts one at a time, shaking until well coated. Place floured chicken in hot oil and brown on each side, about 5 to 7 minutes per side. Transfer browned chicken to a 3 quart casserole dish; set aside. Preheat oven to 350 degrees. Add remaining ingredients, except artichokes, to oil and simmer over medium-low heat for 10 minutes. Pour sauce over chicken and bake, uncovered, 50 minutes. Sprinkle artichoke hearts over top and bake, uncovered, 10 more minutes.

"Everyone loves the unique taste. Serve with rice, vegetable and have a stunning entree!"
Karen Tilson   **Riverside Poly High School, Riverside, CA**

ITALIAN VEGETABLE CHICKEN & PASTA
Serves 4

    ½ pound linguine or vermicelli pasta, cooked
    1 cup zucchini halved, sliced
    1 ¼ cups yellow squash, quartered, sliced
    2 tablespoons olive oil
    ½ cup asparagus, cut into 1" pieces
    2 cloves garlic, diced
    ⅓ cup red bell pepper, julienned
    2 green onions, sliced
    ½ cup mushrooms, sliced
    3 Roma tomatoes, diced
    3 chicken breasts, cooked, diced
    2 cups whipping cream or half & half
    1 teaspoon white pepper
    ½ cup Parmesan cheese, freshly shredded

Cook pasta according to package directions; drain and set aside. Stir fry zucchini and yellow squash in olive oil for 1 minute. Add asparagus, garlic, bell pepper, green onions and mushrooms. Stir fry 3 to 4 minutes until they start to soften. Add tomatoes and cooked chicken. Cook 1 to 2 minutes. Add cooked pasta and rewarm. In a separate pan, heat cream until bubbly. Continue to cook approximately 4 to 5 minutes until it starts to reduce. Add white pepper. Pour cream over vegetables and chicken; add cheese and toss. Serve immediately.

"Great summertime dish!"
Sheri Crouse   **Rhodes Junior High School, Mesa, AZ**

LINDA'S CREAMY CHICKEN PASTA
Serves 4 - 5

    2 ½ pounds chicken
    Ranch dressing
    egg noodles
    Garnish: Parmesan cheese, grated

Cut chicken into pieces; rinse and pat dry. Place in a 9" x 13" pan. Pour enough dressing over chicken to coat. Bake at 350 degrees for 35 to 40 minutes. While chicken bakes, prepare noodles according to package directions; drain. Remove chicken when done and place on serving platter. Pour pan drippings and ranch dressing left in pan over cooked, drained noodles. Add extra dressing from bottle if a creamier sauce is desired. Garnish with Parmesan cheese.

Linda Olsen   **Delta High School, Clarksburg, CA**

MANICOTTI
Serves 4 - 6

2 whole chicken breasts, boiled, shredded (reserve broth)
garlic salt and pepper, to taste
1 bottle thick and zesty marinara sauce
1 package Stouffer's Spinach Souffle
½ cup onion, chopped
1 package Stuff-A-Roni
2 cups cheddar cheese, shredded
6 fresh mushrooms, sliced

Cook chicken with enough water to cover until no longer pink; remove from broth and when cool enough to handle, shred into bite-size pieces. Season chicken with garlic salt and pepper. Add small amount of broth to marinara sauce to thin and set aside. Mix shredded chicken with spinach souffle. Add chopped onions. Stuff mixture into Stuff-A-Roni. Pour a small amount of sauce into baking dish. Lay the stuffed pasta in pan. Pour remaining sauce over top. Shred cheddar cheese over top. Sprinkle with mushrooms and bake 1 hour at 350 degrees.

"Easy, fast and tastes great!"

Pat Peck **Folsom High School, Folsom, CA**

MARIE'S BROCCOLI CHICKEN PASTA
Serves 6

16 ounces fettuccini
3 to 4 boneless, skinless chicken breasts, cut into cubes
1 ½ teaspoons Lawry's seasoned salt
1 teaspoon oil
2 tablespoons water
½ cup butter
2 cloves garlic, minced
8 ounces cream cheese
1 ½ to 2 cups half & half
2 ½ cups broccoli florets, steamed

Cook fettuccini according to package directions. While pasta cooks, season chicken with Lawry's and brown in lightly oiled skillet. Remove chicken from skillet. Add water and butter; heat until butter melts. Add garlic and saute. Stir in cream cheese and 1 ½ cups half & half; stir until cream cheese melts, adding more half & half if sauce is too thick. Drain pasta.In large serving bowl, combine cooked pasta with chicken and broccoli. Pour sauce over and toss well. Serve.

"I had this dish at Marie Callendar's and loved it, so I created my own version!"

Wendy Barnes **Vasquez High School, Acton, CA**

PIZZA CHICKEN
Serves 6

1 (26 ounce) jar spaghetti sauce
2 pounds boneless, skinless chicken breasts
½ cup Italian seasoned bread crumbs
1 egg white
6 slices mozzarella cheese
3 tablespoons olive oil

Easy Italian Favorites

Pour spaghetti sauce into a 13" x 8" baking dish. Rinse chicken breasts and pat dry. Dip in egg white and roll in seasoned bread crumbs. Fry until golden brown in olive oil. Place on top of spaghetti sauce. Bake at 350 degrees for 30 minutes. Remove from oven and cover each breast with a slice of cheese. Bake an additional 5 minutes. Serve with your favorite pasta.

"Takes about 15 minutes to prepare. Looks good and tastes great!"
Rebecca Zavala   **Selma High School, Selma, CA**

RED & GREEN CHICKEN PASTA
Serves 8

4 chicken breasts, cooked and cubed
herbs and spices, as desired
8 ounces rotini pasta
$1/2$ cucumber, sliced, halved
8 cherry tomatoes, halved
6 broccoli florets
1 carrot, sliced
1 bottle Italian dressing

Cook chicken with herbs and spices or use leftover chicken. Cook pasta according to package directions; drain. In large serving dish, combine all ingredients except dressing; toss. Pour dressing over all and toss again. Serve hot or cold.

"When pomegranates are in season, a few seeds thrown into this dish are tasty!
This recipe can be served hot or cold, with the vegetables cooked or raw!"
Laura Carroll   **La Quinta High School, Westminster, CA**

RISOTTO CHICKEN

2 to 4 tablespoons olive oil, divided
2 boneless chicken breasts, cubed
1 cup onion, chopped, divided
3 cloves garlic, minced
salt and pepper, to taste
$1/4$ cup sun-dried tomatoes in oil, drained, chopped
2 to 3 tablespoons fresh herbs, chopped
    (basil, rosemary, thyme, oregano, parsley)
1 $1/2$ cups arborio rice
$1/2$ cup dry white wine
4 to 6 cups hot chicken broth
$1/2$ cup Parmesan cheese, shredded

Heat 1 to 2 tablespoons olive oil in heavy skillet. Saute chicken with $1/2$ cup onion and garlic until chicken is opaque and onion is tender. Season with salt and pepper. Stir in tomatoes and herbs. Keep warm over low heat. In another large, heavy skillet, heat 1 to 2 tablespoons olive oil; saute rice until lightly browned. Add wine and stir until absorbed. Stir in hot chicken broth, 1 cup at a time, stirring until most of the broth is absorbed before adding next cup. Continue adding broth until all 6 cups (or more) have been absorbed and rice is tender, but not mushy. Season with salt and pepper, to taste. Stir in Parmesan cheese.

"I like using a mixture of fresh herbs. I also add fresh vegetables, like asparagus and
mushrooms, if available. Saute vegetables and keep warm with
chicken mixture or use leftover, cooked vegetables."
Laura de la Motte   **Turlock High School, Turlock, CA**

70

SAUTÉED CHICKEN BREAST TARRAGON

Serves 4

        3 tablespoons olive oil
        4 boneless, skinless chicken breast halves
        1/2 cup chicken broth or water
        2 to 3 cloves garlic, crushed
        1 to 2 tablespoons butter
        1 to 2 tablespoons fresh tarragon, chopped
        salt and pepper, to taste

In a heavy skillet, heat olive oil until very hot. Dry chicken breasts thoroughly. Place in skillet, being careful not to crowd them. Saute until well browned. Turn chicken over and brown other side; remove from pan and set aside. Stir in chicken broth or water and reheat until boiling. Carefully scrape pan to remove bits from bottom of pan; boil until mixture is reduced by half. Add fresh garlic, butter, tarragon, salt and pepper to taste. Place chicken breasts back into pan to warm. Serve immediately.

"This is an excellent accompaniment to fettuccini Alfredo. My husband lived in northern Italy for 2 years. This is one of his favorite once-in-a-lifetime dishes. He brought this recipe back with him along with a pasta machine."

Pam Bonilla   **Valley View High School, Moreno Valley, CA**

SUZIE'S ITALIAN CHICKEN

Serves 4

        1/2 cup bacon, chopped
        1 1/2 pounds boneless, skinless chicken breasts
        4 to 6 (medium) Roma tomatoes, seeded, chopped
        1/2 cup dry sherry or chicken broth
        1 tablespoon dry Italian seasoning
        1/8 teaspoon cayenne pepper
        4 cloves garlic, minced
        1 pound fettuccini, hot, cooked
        1 tablespoon butter
        1/2 cup Parmesan cheese, grated

In large frying pan, cook bacon until crisp; remove. Discard all but 1 tablespoon bacon grease. Add chicken and cook, stirring until browned. Remove chicken. Add tomatoes, sherry or broth, seasonings and garlic. Bring to a boil, then simmer 5 to 10 minutes or until most of the liquid has evaporated. Return chicken to pan, stirring until heated. Cook pasta according to package directions; drain. Toss with butter. Place on serving platter. Pour chicken mixture over cooked pasta, top with crumbled bacon and cheese.

"You can make it for an army as easily as for a family, since it doubles or triples easily. And it only takes 20 minutes."

Peggy Goyak   **Birmingham High School, Van Nuys, CA**

It is rude in Italy to twirl your spaghetti in a spoon. You use the side of your bowl.

Dale Sheehan   **Santana HS, Santee, CA**

TORTELLINI CHICKEN PRIMAVERA
Serves 6

1 ½ to 2 pounds boneless, skinless chicken breast meat, cubed
2 to 3 cloves garlic, minced
½ tablespoon dried basil
1 ½ cups water
3 cups tortellini
1 container pesto sauce
3 to 4 Roma tomatoes, chopped
1 red bell pepper, cut into 1" pieces
1 yellow bell pepper, cut into 1" pieces
1 zucchini, sliced
Garnish: Parmesan cheese, shredded

In large Dutch oven, stew chicken, garlic and basil with water. Cook over medium-high heat until all of the water evaporates. In a separate pan, cook pasta as directed on package until al dente; drain. In large pasta serving dish, toss pasta, chicken and pesto sauce with fresh, cut up vegetables. Sprinkle with Parmesan cheese.

"Yummy! A year round favorite dish of my family."

Elizabeth DeMars　　　　　　　**West Hills High School, Santee, CA**

TURKETTI
Serves 4 - 6

1 ¼ cups spaghetti, broken into 2" pieces
1 ½ to 2 cups cooked turkey, cut into chunks
½ cup cooked ham, diced (optional)
¼ cup green pepper, minced
1 can cream of chicken soup
½ cup turkey or chicken broth
⅛ teaspoon celery salt
⅛ teaspoon pepper
½ cup onion, grated
1 ½ cups cheddar cheese, grated
salt and pepper, to taste

Preheat oven to 350 degrees. Cook spaghetti until barely tender; drain. Combine with remaining ingredients except ½ cup grated cheddar cheese. Toss lightly and season to taste with salt and pepper. Pour into a 1 ½ quart casserole dish. Sprinkle with remaining cheddar cheese and bake, covered, 35 minutes.

"This is a great way to use up the end of the turkey. Chicken can be substituted. Add a salad and bread for a quick and easy dinner."

Paula Schaefer　　　　　　**Garside Junior High School, Las Vegas, NV**

For creamy risotto, stir in a pat of butter and a few tablespoons heavy cream after all the broth is absorbed.

Laura de la Motte　　　　　　**Turlock HS, Turlock, CA**

Beef & Lamb

CALIFORNIA CASSEROLE
Serves 6
- 1 ½ pounds ground beef
- 1 teaspoon garlic salt
- 1 teaspoon oregano
- 1 teaspoon sugar
- 3 cups tomato sauce
- 1 cup tomato paste
- 8 ounces egg noodles
- 1 tablespoon margarine
- 4 ounces sour cream
- 3 ounces cream cheese
- 1 (small) can olives, chopped
- 1 cup cheddar cheese, shredded

Cook ground beef; drain. Add garlic salt, oregano, sugar, tomato sauce and tomato paste; simmer 15 minutes. Prepare egg noodles according to package directions; drain and toss with margarine. Mix together sour cream, cream cheese and olives. In a deep casserole dish, place 1 cup meat sauce mixture, noodles, remaining meat sauce and cream cheese mixture. Top with cheddar cheese and bake at 350 degrees 15 minutes, or until hot.

Deborah Weiss   **Ayala High School, Chino Hills, CA**

CANNELLONI
Serves 8
Filling:
- 1 (10 ounce) package frozen spinach, chopped, thawed
- 1 tablespoon cooking oil
- ¼ cup onion, finely chopped
- 2 cloves garlic, minced
- 1 pound ground beef
- 1 egg
- 2 tablespoons Parmesan cheese, grated
- 1 teaspoon dried Italian seasoning, divided
- ¼ teaspoon salt
- ⅛ teaspoon pepper
Sauce:
- 2 cups tomato sauce
- ⅛ teaspoon salt
- ¼ teaspoon Italian seasoning
- 12 manicotti shells, cooked (without salt or fat)

Filling: Place spinach between paper towels and squeeze until barely moist; set aside. Coat a large skillet with cooking oil; place over medium heat until hot. Add

73

onion and garlic; saute 2 minutes. Add spinach; saute 1 minute. Place mixture in large bowl and set aside. Cook ground beef in skillet over medium heat until browned, stirring to crumble. Drain and pat dry with paper towels. Add to spinach mixture. Add egg, Parmesan, Italian seasoning, salt and pepper; stir well and set aside.

Sauce: Combine tomato sauce, salt and Italian seasoning in a bowl, stirring well. Spread 1 cup over bottom of 13" x 9" x 2" baking dish. Stuff each shell with $1/3$ cup spinach mixture and arrange on top of tomato sauce. Sprinkle with remaining 3 tablespoons Parmesan cheese. Cover and bake at 375 degrees for 30 minutes or until thoroughly heated.

Jill Burnham　　　　　**Bloomington High School, Bloomington, CA**

CHEESY-CORN CASSEROLE
Serves 6 - 8

2 to 3 cups noodles, cooked
1 pound ground beef
$1/2$ onion, chopped
1 can tomato soup
1 (small) can creamed corn
1 (small) can ripe olives, sliced
1 (small) can mushrooms, sliced
2 cups cheddar cheese, grated

Prepare noodles according to package directions; set aside. Brown ground beef; drain excess fat. Add onions and brown lightly. Add soup, cooked noodles, corn, olives and mushrooms. Simmer 10 to 15 minutes. Stir in half of the cheese. Place in a 2 quart casserole and top with remaining cheese. Bake at 400 degrees for 30 minutes.

"Tastes wonderful. Easy to make. Kids love it!"

Olga Sarouhan　　　　　**Edison High School, Huntington Beach, CA**

EGGPLANT PARMIGIANA
Serves 8

2 tablespoons olive oil
$1/2$ cup onion, chopped
1 clove garlic, minced
1 pound ground beef, lean
1 (1 pound 1 ounce) can Italian-style tomatoes
1 (6 ounce) can tomato sauce
2 teaspoon dried oregano leaves
1 teaspoon dried basil
1 $1/2$ teaspoon salt
$1/4$ teaspoon pepper
1 tablespoons brown sugar
1 cup + 1 tablespoon water, divided
1 (large) eggplant, about 1 $1/2$ pounds
2 eggs, slightly beaten
$1/2$ cup dry bread crumbs
1 $1/4$ cup Parmesan cheese, freshly grated
$1/4$ cup salad oil
8 ounces mozzarella cheese, sliced

In large skillet, saute onion, garlic and ground beef in olive oil until browned, about 5 minutes. Add undrained tomatoes, tomato paste, oregano, basil, salt, pepper, brown sugar and 1 cup water; bring to a boil. Reduce heat; simmer, uncovered, 20 minutes. Wash eggplant; do not peel. Cut crosswise into ½" thick slices. In pie plate, combine eggs with 1 tablespoon water; mix well. On sheet of waxed paper, combine bread crumbs and ½ cup Parmesan cheese, mix well. Dip eggplant slices in egg mixture; then dip into bread crumb mixture, coating evenly. Saute eggplant slices, a few at a time, in hot oil, until golden brown and crisp on both sides, adding oil as needed. Arrange half the eggplant slices in bottom of lightly greased 12" x 9" x 2" baking dish. Sprinkle with half of the remaining Parmesan cheese. Top with half of the mozzarella; cover with half of sauce. Arrange remaining slices over sauce, then remaining Parmesan cheese and tomato sauce. Bake at 350 degrees for 20 minutes. Uncover and top with remaining mozzarella cheese. Bake 20 minutes more, or until mozzarella is melted and lightly browned.

"Make ahead, bake and freeze. This is delicious! Omit the beef for a vegetarian version."

Sue Hope   **Lompoc High School, Lompoc, CA**
Marty Parker   **Poway High School, Poway, CA**

ELIS' CAVATINNI

1 (small) package spiral noodles
1 (small) jar Prego spaghetti sauce
1 can Italian stewed tomatoes
Toppings: pepperoni, diced black olives,
     sliced mushrooms (canned or fresh)
mozzarella cheese, shredded

Cook noodles according to package directions; drain well. Combine noodles with spaghetti sauce and stewed tomatoes; pour into casserole dish. Stir in desired toppings and heat in oven at 350 degrees, until warmed through, about 15 to 20 minutes. Top with mozzarella and serve.

"You can serve from the pan and sprinkle cheese on top."

Eloise Hatfield   **Poston Junior High School, Mesa, AZ**

EXTRA EASY LASAGNA

Serves 8

¾ pound ground beef
3 cups spaghetti sauce
6 dry lasagna noodles
1 (15 ounce) carton ricotta cheese
2 cups mozzarella cheese, shredded
¼ cup water

Preheat oven to 375 degrees. Cook ground beef; drain excess fat. Combine with spaghetti sauce and heat through. In a 2 quart oblong dish, spread 1 ½ cups sauce in bottom. Top with 3 noodles, half of the ricotta cheese and half of mozzarella. Repeat layers. Slowly pour ¼ cup water around inside edge of dish. Cover and bake 45 minutes. Uncover and bake 10 minutes more. Let stand 10 minutes before serving.

"This is an easy Italian favorite and tastes great with Mama Bella garlic bread."

Melissa Webb   **Lakewood High School, Lakewood, CA**

FLORENTINE MANICOTTI

Serves 6 - 7

3 packages manicotti noodles
½ cup onion, chopped
1 clove garlic, minced
1 pound ground beef
1 tablespoon margarine
2 (10 ounce) packages chopped spinach, drained
1 pound ricotta or cottage cheese
3 eggs, slightly beaten
1 pound mozzarella cheese, shredded
½ cup Parmesan cheese, grated
1 teaspoon salt
dash pepper
1 tablespoon lemon juice
1 pound cheddar cheese, shredded
1 (large) jar spaghetti sauce

Prepare noodles according to package directions. Saute onion, garlic, beef and margarine until tender. Combine with spinach, ricotta or cottage cheese, eggs, mozzarella, Parmesan, salt, pepper and lemon juice; blend well. Fill noodles and place in 9" x 13" pan. Pour spaghetti sauce over noodles. Sprinkle with shredded cheddar cheese. Cover with foil and bake at 350 degrees for 40 to 60 minutes.

"Always a big hit! One of my family's favorites."

Roberta Hawkes   **A. B. Miller High School, Fontana, CA**

Season sausage with garlic, oregano, basil and onion salt if it is not pre-seasoned Italian sausage. While studying Italian Cuisine, we found that before refrigeration, meat was kept with large amounts of salt to help preserve it. Because of this, chefs made wonderful sauces full of delicate flavors and scents to cover the saltiness of the meat.

Gerry Henderson   **Temple City HS, Temple City, CA**

GARLIC TOMATO SAUCE & MEATBALLS

Serves 4

Sauce:
3 to 4 tablespoons olive oil
$\frac{1}{2}$ (medium) onion, chopped
4 to 5 cloves garlic, minced
1 tablespoons fresh Italian parsley, chopped
1 (8 ounce) can tomato sauce + scant can of water
1 (6 ounce) can tomato paste + scant can of water
1 to 2 teaspoons dried oregano
$\frac{1}{4}$ teaspoon dried sweet basil
1 bay leaf
$\frac{1}{4}$ to $\frac{1}{2}$ teaspoon dried Italian seasoning
$\frac{1}{4}$ to $\frac{1}{2}$ teaspoon sugar
salt and pepper, to taste

Meatballs:
$\frac{1}{2}$ pound ground beef (30% fat)
$\frac{1}{4}$ pound ground pork (optional)
2 cloves garlic, minced
1 egg, beaten
2 to 3 tablespoons water
1 cup plain dry breadcrumbs (add more as needed)
2 teaspoons Parmesan cheese, grated
$\frac{1}{4}$ teaspoon dried oregano
$\frac{1}{2}$ teaspoon fresh parsley, chopped
$\frac{1}{2}$ teaspoon salt
$\frac{1}{4}$ teaspoon pepper

Sauce: Heat olive oil in a medium saucepan on high. Add onions and saute 1 minute. Turn down heat to medium-high. Cook about 9 minutes or until lightly browned. Add garlic, saute about 5 minutes, or until both are golden brown, not burned. Add fresh parsley and saute just a few seconds. Add tomato sauce and paste. Fill cans with equal parts of water (scant) and add to the sauce. Stir well until all lumps are dissolved. Add dried herbs by crushing between your two hands. Add sugar, salt and pepper. (You may add more herbs and seasonings to your taste.) Reduce heat to low and simmer 45 minutes to 1 hour. Add cooked meatballs.

Meatballs: Mix ground beef with ground pork until well blended. Add remaining ingredients and mix well. Shape into 1 $\frac{1}{2}$ to 2" balls. Heat frying pan with about 1 to 2 tablespoons olive oil. Place meatballs in pan and cook over medium-high heat, turning when meat loosens from pan. When done, remove and drain on paper towels. Add to sauce, stirring carefully.

To serve with cooked pasta: Place drained pasta in a pot. Toss with $\frac{1}{2}$ cup sauce, coating the pasta with a light coating of sauce. Serve on plates and drizzle with a little more sauce on top. Sprinkle and garnish with fresh chopped basil and grated Parmesan/Romano cheese. Any reserved sauce can be placed in a sauceboat or server.

"This is my family's version on my mother's side, from Sicily. The secret to good sauce is not to burn the onions or garlic. Use Hunt's Sauce and Paste. This is the best tasting sauce you will ever eat. In addition, I also use this same sauce for my pizzas."

JoAnn Himmelberger   **Santa Ana High School, Santa Ana, CA**

GOURMET LASAGNA
Serves 10

2 pounds lean ground beef
2 cloves garlic minced
1 teaspoon garlic salt
6 (8 ounce) cans tomato sauce
1 (8 ounce) package wide noodles
8 green onions, chopped
1 (8 ounce) package cream cheese
2 cups sour cream
1 pound mozzarella cheese, shredded
½ cup Parmesan cheese, grated

Brown ground beef with garlic, garlic salt and tomato sauce. Cover and simmer 20 minutes. Cook and drain noodles according to package directions. Spread half of the noodles in a shallow dish. Blend green onions into cream cheese and sour cream. Spread one third of green onion mixture over noodles in baking dish. Add a layer of meat. Repeat layers. Top with mozzarella and Parmesan cheeses. Bake at 350 degrees for 20 to 30 minutes.

Audrey Birch   **Parras Middle School, Redondo Beach, CA**

I-ONLY-EAT-PIZZA CASSEROLE
Serves 10

12 ounces wide noodles
1 ½ pounds ground beef
3 cups pizza sauce
salt and pepper, to taste
2 cups mozzarella cheese, grated

Cook noodles in salted water 3 to 4 minutes; drain. Brown ground beef and drain excess fat. Mix beef with pizza sauce; season to taste with salt and pepper. Put half of the noodles in a greased 9" x 13" dish. Cover with half of the sauce and half of the cheese. Repeat layers. Bake at 350 degrees 30 minutes.

"Great for that ski or river trip when you need a big casserole to share."

Lynda Ruth   **La Mirada High School, La Mirada, CA**

ITALIAN CRESCENT BAKE
Serves 8 - 10

1 pound ground beef
½ cup onion, chopped
1 cup fresh mushrooms, sliced
salt and pepper, to taste
8 ounces tomato sauce
1 cup cheddar cheese, grated
1 tube crescent rolls
½ cup sour cream
¼ teaspoon oregano
¼ teaspoon basil

Brown ground beef with onion and mushrooms; drain excess fat. Season with salt and pepper. Add tomato sauce. Pour into a 9" x 13" pan, top with cheese. Separate package crescent rolls. Mix sour cream with oregano and basil. Spread sour cream mixture on each roll. Roll up crescent roll, starting at the wide end. Place rolls on top of meat mixture. Bake at 375 degrees for approximately 2 minutes, until rolls are lightly browned.

"Winning recipe in our Nutrition Class Cook off - quick and easy."
Brenda Hill   **Folsom High School, Folsom, CA**

ITALIAN MEATBALLS & SAUCE
Serves 6 - 8

2 eggs, beaten
¼ cup milk
½ cup dried bread crumbs, garlic & herb flavored
2 tablespoons Parmesan cheese, grated
1 teaspoon salt
¼ teaspoon pepper
½ teaspoon garlic powder
1 pound ground beef
½ pound bulk Italian sausage
1 (15 ounce) can tomato sauce
1 (6 ounce) can tomato paste
1 small onion, chopped
½ cup beef broth
⅓ cup water
4 cloves garlic, minced
1 teaspoon dried oregano
½ teaspoon pepper
16 ounces cooked spaghetti
Garnish: Parmesan cheese, grated

In a large mixing bowl, combine eggs and milk; add bread crumbs, cheese, salt, pepper and garlic powder. Add beef and sausage and mix well. Shape into 1" balls. Brown in large skillet, then transfer to slow cooker. Combine tomato sauce and paste, onion, broth, water and remaining seasonings; pour over meatballs. Cover and cook on low 4 to 5 hours. Serve over cooked noodles. Sprinkle with Parmesan cheese, if desired.

"I got this recipe from Taste of Home's Quick Cooking. *This is a family favorite!"*
Astrid Curfman   **Newcomb Academy, Long Beach, CA**

ITALIAN NOODLE CASSEROLE
Serves 8

1 (8 ounce) package thin egg noodles
1 clove garlic
1 ½ pounds lean ground beef
1 tablespoon butter
3 (8 ounce) cans tomato sauce
salt and pepper, to taste
1 tablespoon sugar
1 cup cottage cheese
1 (8 ounce) package cream cheese
¼ cup sour cream
⅓ cup onion, chopped
¼ cup green pepper, chopped
1 cup cheddar cheese, grated

Easy Italian Favorites

Cook noodles according to package directions; drain. Preheat oven to 350 degrees. Brown ground beef and garlic in butter. Add tomato sauce, salt, pepper and sugar; set aside. Blend together cream cheese and cottage cheese. Stir in sour cream, onion and green pepper. In a greased 9" x 13" pan, put half of the cooked noodles, then a layer of cheese, then rest of noodles. Cover with ground beef mixture and top with cheddar cheese. Bake 30 minutes.

Sharron Maurice   **Blythe Middle School, Blythe, CA**

ITALIAN POT ROAST
Serves 9 - 12

> 3 tablespoons oil
> 1 (4 ounce) can mushrooms, sliced
> 2 (medium) onions, sliced
> 3 to 4 pound chuck roast
> $\frac{1}{4}$ cup flour
> 1 (#2) can tomatoes
> $\frac{1}{2}$ cup green olives, chopped
> $\frac{1}{2}$ cup chili sauce
> 4 teaspoons Worcestershire sauce
> $\frac{1}{2}$ clove garlic
> $\frac{1}{4}$ teaspoon salt
> $\frac{1}{4}$ teaspoon pepper

Heat oil in heavy roasting pan. Saute mushrooms and onions; remove from oil and set aside. Dredge meat in flour and slowly brown in oil, on all sides. Return mushrooms and onions to pan; add remaining ingredients. Cover tightly and simmer until tender, 2 to 3 hours.

"My sister-in-law's favorite! Nice for covered dish luncheon."

Sonja Tyree   **Ayala High School, Chino Hills, CA**

Italian foods vary greatly by region. In the north, flat, ribbon-shaped pastas served with cream sauces are most popular. In the south, macaroni served with tomato-based sauces are the favorite.

Carol Helmle   **Tokay HS, Lodi, CA**

ITALIAN SPAGHETTI WITH MEATBALLS
Serves 4 - 6

Meatballs:
1 pound ground beef
$\frac{1}{2}$ cup bread crumbs
$\frac{1}{4}$ cup milk
1 teaspoon salt
1 egg
$\frac{1}{4}$ teaspoon oregano
2 tablespoons Parmesan cheese, grated
dash garlic powder
Sauce:
2 (6 ounce) cans tomato paste
2 (8 ounce) cans tomato sauce
3 cups water
2 teaspoons oregano
2 teaspoons parsley flakes
2 cloves garlic, minced
1 teaspoon basil
$\frac{1}{4}$ onion, minced
1 $\frac{1}{2}$ teaspoons sugar
Pasta:
2 teaspoons salt
1 pound spaghetti

Meatballs: Mix the first 8 ingredients together in a bowl. Shape into 1 $\frac{1}{2}$" meatballs. Brown lightly in a heavy skillet, turning carefully to brown on all sides. Remove from pan and set aside.

Sauce: Mix all sauce ingredients in a saucepan; add cooked meatballs and simmer 30 to 40 minutes.

Pasta: Bring 8 to 10 cups water to a boil; add salt and boil spaghetti until al dente. Drain thoroughly. Place pasta on a large platter. Top with meatballs and sauce and serve.

Bonnie Landin   **Garden Grove High School, Garden Grove, CA**

ITALIAN STYLE MEAT LOAF
Serves 8

1 cup Prego spaghetti sauce, divided
2 pounds ground beef
1 $\frac{1}{2}$ cups Pepperidge Farms Herb Seasoned Stuffing
2 eggs, beaten
1 large onion, finely chopped
$\frac{1}{2}$ cup mozzarella cheese, shredded

In a large bowl, mix thoroughly $\frac{1}{2}$ cup spaghetti sauce, beef, stuffing, eggs and onion. In a 2 quart oblong baking dish, firmly shape meat mixture into an 8" x 4" loaf. Bake at 350 degrees for 1 hour, 25 minutes, until meat is no longer pink. Spoon remaining $\frac{1}{2}$ cup spaghetti sauce over meat loaf; sprinkle with cheese. Bake 5 minutes more or until cheese is melted. If desired, garnish with red onions and fresh sage.

"This recipe comes from Prego Easy Italian Recipe Book.*"*

Angela Cruz-Trujillo   **Valley View High School, Moreno Valley, CA**

LAMB & SPINACH MANICOTTI

Serves 8   *Photo opposite page 128*

   1 (5 ounce) box manicotti pasta
Sauce:
   1 ½ pounds ground American lamb
   1 (small) onion, chopped
   ¼ teaspoon pepper
   ½ teaspoon salt
   1 (16 ounce) jar tomato sauce, spaghetti or Italian herb sauce
Stuffing:
   1 tablespoon butter or margarine
   1 (large) onion, finely chopped
   2 cloves garlic, minced
   2 (10 ounce) packages frozen chopped spinach, thawed, drained
   2 eggs, slightly beaten
   ½ teaspoon salt
   1 teaspoon dried oregano leaves
   ½ teaspoon basil leaves, diced
   1 cup ricotta cheese
   1 cup Monterey Jack cheese, grated
   ½ cup Parmesan cheese, grated

Cook pasta according to package directions; drain.

Sauce: Brown ground lamb with onion; drain well. Add tomato sauce, salt and pepper. Simmer 15 to 20 minutes.

Stuffing: Melt butter in skillet; add onion and garlic and cook, stirring constantly, until onion is transparent. Add spinach, cook until moisture has evaporated. Remove from heat. Add eggs, salt, oregano, basil and ricotta. Stuff pasta.

Pour thin layer of sauce in large baking dish. Arrange stuffed manicotti on sauce. Top with remaining sauce, cover with Monterey Jack and Parmesan cheeses. Bake, uncovered, at 350 degrees for 25 to 30 minutes, or until bubbly and completely heated.

American Sheep Industry   **Englewood, CO**

LASAGNA

Serves 6

   1 (12 ounce) can tomato paste
   1 ¾ cups water
   4 tablespoons olive oil
   2 tablespoons spaghetti sauce seasoning
   4 tablespoons wine vinegar
   4 quarts boiling salted water
   ½ pound lasagna noodles (about 10 pieces)
   1 pound ground beef
   1 (16 ounce) carton cottage cheese
   6 ounces mozzarella cheese, thinly sliced
   ⅓ cup Parmesan cheese, grated

Combine tomato paste, water, olive oil, seasoning, wine vinegar; bring to a boil. Cover and simmer while you prepare pasta. Bring salted water to a boil. Slowly add noodles, cooking 15 minutes. Drain and rinse in cold water. Fry ground beef until browned; drain excess fat. Assemble in 9" x 13" pan: put a layer of noodles in bottom, spoon over 4 to 5 spoonfuls cottage cheese and one third of the meat. Cover with tomato sauce and thin slices of mozzarella, using one fourth of each. Repeat layers, topping with sauce and grated Parmesan cheese. Bake at 350 degrees for 30 to 35 minutes. Cut into squares.

*"This is a favorite of my students for our Italian lab.
We serve garlic bread, a tossed salad, and it's a hit every time!"*

Sandy Robertson   **Whittier High School, Whittier, CA**

MICROWAVE LASAGNA
Serves 4

1/2 pound ground beef
1 (16 ounce) jar spaghetti sauce
1/2 teaspoon salt
1/4 cup water
4 ounces uncooked lasagna noodles
7 1/2 ounces ricotta cheese
1 cup mozzarella cheese, shredded
2 tablespoons Parmesan cheese, grated

Place ground beef in a 1 quart casserole dish. Break meat apart and microwave 5 to 6 minutes on HIGH (100% power). Stir and break meat apart halfway through cooking; drain excess fat. Combine cooked beef with sauce, salt and water. Microwave 5 minutes on HIGH, or until hot. In a 8" x 8" glass dish, place 1/3 of the sauce, 1/2 of the uncooked noodles, all of the ricotta cheese and all of the mozzarella cheese; another 1/3 of the sauce, remaining noodles and remaining sauce over top. Cover with two layers of plastic wrap. Microwave on HIGH for 12 minutes. Turn dish and microwave on MEDIUM (50% power) 10 to 15 minutes. Let stand, covered, for 5 minutes before serving. Top with Parmesan cheese.

Liz Aschenbrenner   **Sierra High School, Manteca, CA**

MICROWAVE STUFFED BELL PEPPERS
Serves 6

1 cup rice, cooked (brown or white)
6 large bell peppers
1 pound lean ground beef
1/4 cup Parmesan cheese, grated
1/2 cup onion, chopped
1/8 teaspoon garlic powder
1 (15 ounce) can tomato sauce, divided
3/4 cup mozzarella cheese, shredded

Prepare rice according to package directions; set aside. Cut thin slice from stem end of each pepper; remove seeds and membranes; rinse and set aside. Mix together uncooked ground beef, cooked rice, Parmesan, onion, garlic powder and 1 cup of tomato sauce. Stuff peppers evenly with meat mixture. Place peppers, cut sides up, in an ungreased 9" or 10" glass pie plate. Pour remaining sauce over peppers. Cover with plastic wrap and microwave on HIGH 15 minutes. Top with mozzarella cheese. Allow to stand 5 minutes before serving.

Ellen Gordon   **Colton High School, Colton, CA**

MOUNTAIN GIRL'S PASTA DELIGHT
Serves 4

3 to 4 links hot Italian sausage
3 to 4 tablespoons olive oil
7 to 9 fresh sage leaves, chopped
3 cup mostaccioli
1 cup peas, frozen
$\frac{1}{2}$ cup Parmesan cheese, freshly grated

Crumble sausage and saute until browned, in 3 to 4 tablespoons olive oil; drain excess fat. Add sage and saute 2 to 3 minutes. Boil mostaccioli according to package directions; drain. Add pasta to sausage along with frozen peas. Cover and simmer 5 minutes, stirring 1 to 2 times. Place finished meal on platter; cover with Parmesan cheese and serve.

"Recipe comes from a very dear Italian friend, Victor Puglisi, who's very protective of the family's old school secrets. I can guarantee this will become one of your family favorites!"
Connie Sweet   Rim of the World High School, Lake Arrowhead, CA

MY KIDS' FAVORITE CASSEROLE
Serves 6

$\frac{1}{2}$ pound lean ground beef
7 ounces small elbow macaroni
16 ounces spaghetti sauce (or more to taste)
1 cup sharp cheddar cheese, grated
$\frac{1}{4}$ cup Parmesan cheese, grated

Crumble and cook beef thoroughly; drain excess fat. Cook macaroni according to package directions; drain. Mix macaroni, ground beef, spaghetti sauce and cheddar cheese together and spread into casserole dish. Sprinkle with Parmesan cheese. Microwave on HIGH 8 minutes, turning halfway through cooking, until hot. NOTE: Keeps well in refrigerator. Bring to room temperature before microwave cooking.

"This is an easy, inexpensive comfort food which serves 6 kids of any age!."
Sue Ellen Warren   Bellflower High School, Bellflower, CA

NEVER-FAIL MEATBALLS
Serves 4

1 pound ground beef, 22% fat (lower fat ground beef
     makes meat balls too dry)
$\frac{1}{3}$ cup milk
$\frac{1}{3}$ cup bread crumbs
1 egg
2 tablespoons parsley
salt and pepper, to taste
1 jar spaghetti sauce, heated

Combine all ingredients in a large bowl and mix well with an electric mixture until well blended. Shape into golf ball size meatballs. Drop into hot spaghetti sauce. Cover and cook for at least 1 hour.

"Mixing with the electric mixer is the secret to making these meatballs the best."
Carol Steele   La Paz Intermediate School, Mission Viejo, CA

NO-FUSS BEEF & SPINACH LASAGNA

Serves 12   *Photo opposite page 65*

1 pound ground beef
$\frac{1}{4}$ teaspoon salt
1 jar or can (26 to 30 ounce) prepared lowfat spaghetti sauce
1 (14.5 ounce) can Italian-style tomatoes, diced, undrained
$\frac{1}{4}$ teaspoon ground red pepper
1 (15 ounce) carton part-skim ricotta cheese
1 (10 ounce) package frozen chopped spinach, thawed, well drained
$\frac{1}{4}$ cup Parmesan cheese, grated
1 egg, beaten
10 lasagna noodles, uncooked
1 $\frac{1}{2}$ cups part-skim mozzarella cheese, shredded

Heat oven to 375 degrees. In large nonstick skillet, brown ground beef over medium heat 8 to 10 minutes or until no longer pink. Pour off drippings. Season with salt; add spaghetti sauce, tomatoes and red pepper, stirring to combine. Set aside. Meanwhile, in medium bowl, combine ricotta cheese, spinach, Parmesan cheese and egg. Spread 2 cups beef sauce over bottom of 9" x 13" baking dish. Arrange 5 lasagna noodles in single layer, completely covering bottom of dish; press noodles into sauce. Spread entire ricotta cheese mixture on top of noodles; sprinkle with 1 cup mozzarella cheese and top with 2 cups beef sauce. Arrange remaining noodles in single layer; press lightly into sauce. Top with remaining sauce. Bake 45 minutes or until noodles are tender. Sprinkle remaining mozzarella cheese on top; tent lightly with aluminum foil. Let stand 15 minutes before cutting into 12 squares.

"The noodles cook during the baking."

National Cattlemen's Beef Association   **Chicago, IL**

The old Italians used to dip their anise cookies in wine, probably to soften a bit since the cookie is a tad crisp.

Maria Fregulia   **Lassen UHS, Susanville, CA**

ORLANDO MOSTACCIOLI AND MEATBALLS

Serves 8 - 12

Sauce:
1 to 2 pounds mild sausage
   (may substitute ½ hot and ½ sweet sausage)
1 tablespoon parsley
2 teaspoons oregano
pinch of basil, if desired
6 (large) cloves garlic, minced
1 teaspoon salt
3 (large) cans tomato puree
3 (small) cans tomato paste
1 onion, whole
Meatballs:
2 ½ to 3 pounds ground beef
1 (large) package meat loaf seasoning mix
2 cloves garlic, finely chopped
1 tablespoon parsley
salt and pepper, to taste
3 eggs, beaten
4 slices bread
½ cup milk
¾ cup bread crumbs
1 small can Parmesan cheese, grated
Optional:
chicken hearts and gizzards
Pasta:
1 to 2 pounds mostaccioli (may substitute spaghetti)

Sauce: Brown sausage in large pot. Cook, covered, about 30 minutes. Remove sausage, leaving most fat for flavor. Add parsley, oregano, basil (if desired for sweetness), garlic and salt; stir. Add tomato puree and tomato paste; mix well. Fill both puree and paste cans with water and add to sauce; mix well. Add whole onion (which will be removed just before serving). Simmer at least 2 hours.

Meatballs: In a large bowl, mix together ground beef, seasoning mix, garlic, parsley, salt, pepper and eggs. In a small bowl, soak each slice of bread in the milk. Squeeze out excess milk and break bread apart into small pieces. Combine bread, bread crumbs and Parmesan cheese. Add to ground beef and mix thoroughly. Shape into small balls and cook in frying pan or bake in 350 degree oven for 40 minutes. Add to sauce to serve.

Optional: Squeeze blood out of hole in hearts. Cut off excess fat from gizzards. Boil hearts and gizzards in water or broth until fork inserts easily. Add to sauce to serve.

Pasta: Prepare pasta according to package directions. Drain and rinse well with hot water. Return pasta to pan and stir in a small amount of sauce to prevent sticking. When serving, top with sauce.

"This was the Sunday meal for my husband's Italian family, along with mushrooms fried in garlic and oil. This recipe is in memory of his mother, Kate and Aunt Dolly."

Gerry Henderson   **Temple City High School, Temple City, CA**

Pepperoni Hot Dish
Serves

7 ounces spaghetti, cooked and drained
1 egg, beaten
$\frac{1}{2}$ cup milk
1 $\frac{1}{2}$ pounds ground beef, cooked and drained
1 (large) jar spaghetti sauce
2 cups mozzarella cheese, shredded
4 ounces pepperoni slices

Prepare spaghetti according to package directions.Spread cooked spaghetti in bottom of a 9" x 12" pan. Cook ground beef over medium heat 8 to 10 minutes or until no longer pink. Drain excess fat; set aside. Combine beaten egg with milk; pour over spaghetti. Cover with ground beef. Pour spaghetti sauce evenly over top. Sprinkle cheese and pepperoni over top and refrigerate overnight. Preheat oven to 350 degrees. Bake, covered, 1 hour; remove cover and bake additional 15 minutes.

Linda Mastre   **Durango High School, Las Vegas, NV**

Rigatoni Special
Serves 6

12 ounces rigatoni noodles, cooked
1 pound ground beef
$\frac{1}{2}$ green pepper, chopped
1 (8 ounce) can stewed tomatoes
1 (16 ounce) can spaghetti sauce
1 pound Italian Sausage
1 cup cheddar cheese, grated

Prepare noodles according to package directions; set aside. Brown ground beef; drain excess fat. Add chopped green peppers, stewed tomatoes and spaghetti sauce; simmer 15 minutes. In separate pan, cook Italian sausage; drain on paper towels. Slice sausage and add to beef mixture. Mix meat with cooked noodles and place in casserole dish. Sprinkle cheese on top and bake at 350 degrees 10 to 15 minutes, or until cheese is melted.

Linda Vincent   **Turlock High School, Turlock, CA**

Roman Holiday
Serves 8 - 12

2 pounds ground beef
1 to 2 cloves garlic, minced
salt and seasoned pepper, to taste
dash Worcestershire sauce
chili powder, to taste
2 cups white onion, chopped
2 cups celery, chopped
2 (medium) green peppers, chopped
2 (8 ounce) cans mushroom stems and pieces
2 (large) cans seasoned tomatoes (reserve juice from 1 can)
1 (small) can seasoned tomatoes
3 cups (medium sized) noodles, partially cooked

Brown ground beef with garlic, salt, pepper, Worcestershire, chili powder and onions;

set aside. Saute celery and green peppers. Stir in mushrooms. Combine with meat mixture and spread in a 14" x 10" x 2 ½" glass dish. Add tomatoes. Bake 1 hour at 325 degrees. Remove from oven; add partially cooked noodles and pour enough reserved liquid from tomatoes over casserole to keep it from getting too dry. Return to oven and bake 30 minutes more.

"From my mother, Liz Richards, whose recipe was a handful of this and that. We got the recipe as close as we could to Home Ec. standards."

Gayle Grigg   **Hendrix Junior High School, Chandler, AZ**

SLOP LOLLY
Serves 4

½ pound ground beef
1 (14.5 ounce) can stewed tomatoes
2 tablespoons dried minced onions
½ teaspoon salt
½ teaspoon chili powder
¼ teaspoon pepper
⅛ teaspoon sugar
½ cup elbow macaroni, uncooked

In a skillet brown beef; drain excess fat. Add tomatoes and seasonings; bring to a boil. Reduce heat and simmer 5 minutes. Stir in macaroni; cover and simmer 15 minutes more. Uncover, simmer until macaroni is tender and sauce has thickened.

Jennifer Walker   **Bloomington High School, Bloomington, CA**

SLOW COOKER LASAGNA
Serves 6 - 8

1 pound ground beef
1 (large) onion, chopped
2 cloves garlic, minced
1 (29 ounce) can tomato sauce
1 cup water
1 can tomato paste
1 teaspoon salt
1 teaspoon dried oregano
1 (8 ounce) package no cook lasagna noodles
4 cups (16 ounces) mozzarella cheese, shredded
1 ½ cups (12 ounces) small curd cottage cheese
½ cup Parmesan cheese, grated

In a skillet, cook beef, onion and garlic over medium heat until meat is no longer pink; drain excess fat. Add tomato sauce, water, tomato paste, salt and oregano; mix well. Spread ¼ of the meat sauce in an ungreased 5 quart slow cooker. Arrange a third of the noodles over sauce, breaking noodles if necessary. Combine cheese; spoon one third of the mixture over noodles. Repeat layers twice. Top with remaining sauce. Cover and cook on low 4 to 5 hours. Test noodles for tenderness.

"I use this recipe on those busy school days, but it can also be used for company"

Shirley Blough   **Hillside Middle School, Simi Valley, CA**

SPAGHETTI PIE
Serves 6

6 ounces spaghetti
2 tablespoons butter or margarine
2 eggs, beaten (or ½ cup egg substitute)
⅓ cup Parmesan cheese, grated
1 cup cottage cheese
½ cup onion, chopped
¼ cup green pepper, chopped
1 pound lean ground beef
1 (8 ounce) can tomatoes, diced
1 (6 ounce) can tomato paste
1 teaspoon sugar
1 teaspoon oregano
½ teaspoon garlic salt
½ cup mozzarella cheese, shredded

Cook spaghetti according to package directions; drain. Stir butter or margarine into hot spaghetti; stir in eggs and Parmesan cheese. Form spaghetti mixture into a crust by pressing into a 10" pie plate. Spread with cottage cheese. In skillet, cook ground meat, onion and green pepper until meat is brown and vegetables are tender; drain fat. Stir in undrained tomatoes, tomato paste, sugar, oregano and garlic salt; heat through. Spoon meat mixture into spaghetti crust and bake, uncovered at 350 degrees for 20 minutes. Sprinkle with mozzarella cheese and bake 5 minutes more, or until cheese melts.

"You can substitute the meat sauce with about 2 ½ cups prepared spaghetti sauce."

Margene Rich   **Fairfield High School, Fairfield, CA**
Cindi Gavin   **Rancho Bernardo High School, San Diego, CA**

STUFFED MANICOTTI
Serves 6 - 8

1 clove garlic, crushed
½ cup onion, chopped
1 teaspoon margarine, melted
½ pound ground beef
½ pound Italian sausage
1 teaspoon flour
1 (29 ounce) can tomato sauce
1 can tomatoes, chopped
1 cup mushrooms, sliced
1 ½ teaspoons salt
½ teaspoon pepper
1 tablespoon sugar
1 teaspoon crushed oregano
¾ teaspoon Italian seasoning
12 to 14 manicotti shells
Filling:
15 ounces ricotta cheese
1 cup mozzarella cheese, grated
½ cup Parmesan cheese, grated
1 egg, beaten

Easy Italian Favorites

Saute garlic and onion in melted margarine. Add ground beef and sausage; brown, breaking up meats. Drain excess fat. Stir in flour, tomato sauce, canned tomatoes, mushrooms and all seasonings. Simmer, uncovered, 15 minutes, stirring ocassionally. Combine filling ingredients in a bowl. Stuff uncooked manicotti shells with cheese filling. Cover bottom of a 9" x 13" baking dish with meat sauce; arrange stuffed shells on top. Cover shells completely with remaining meat sauce. Cover dish with foil and bake at 375 degrees for 40 to 45 minutes.

Diana Lee   **David A. Brown Middle School, Wildomar, CA**

VEAL PICCATA

Serves 4   *Photo opposite page 97*

    1 pound veal leg cutlets, cut $\frac{1}{8}$" to $\frac{1}{4}$" thick
    2 tablespoons all-purpose flour
    $\frac{1}{2}$ teaspoon salt
    $\frac{1}{8}$ teaspoon paprika
    $\frac{1}{8}$ teaspoon ground white pepper
    1 tablespoon olive oil
    Lemon-Caper Sauce:
    $\frac{2}{3}$ cup dry white wine
    2 tablespoons fresh lemon juice
    2 teaspoons capers, drained
    1 teaspoon butter

Pound veal cutlets to $\frac{1}{8}$" thickness, if necessary. Combine flour, salt, paprika and white pepper. Lightly coat both sides of cutlets with flour mixture. In large nonstick skillet, heat half of the oil over medium heat until hot. Add half of the cutlets; cook 3 to 4 minutes or until cooked through, turning once. Remove cutlets; keep warm. Repeat with remaining oil and cutlets. Add wine and lemon juice to skillet; cook and stir until browned bits attached to skillet are dissolved and liquid thickens slightly. Remove from heat; stir in capers and butter. Spoon sauce over cutlets.

National Cattlemen's Beef Association   **Chicago, IL**

VEAL SCALLOPPINI & WHITE WINE SAUCE

Serves 4 - 6

    1 $\frac{1}{2}$ pounds veal scallopini, cut $\frac{1}{4}$" thick
    $\frac{1}{2}$ cup all-purpose flour
    salt and freshly ground pepper, to taste
    4 tablespoons butter
    1 tablespoon olive oil
    1 cup chardonnay wine
    1 tablespoon fresh parsley, chopped
    3 cups cooked rice

Dust each piece of veal with flour. Season with salt and pepper. Heat 3 tablespoons butter and oil in large, heavy skillet. When butter foams, add veal. Cook over high heat until lightly golden on both sides, about 2 minutes. Transfer to a plate. Add remaining tablespoon butter to skillet, then add wine. Deglaze pan by stirring to dissolve meat juices attached to the bottom of the skillet. When wine is reduced by half, add parsley and stir to incorporate. Return veal to the skillet and mix gently and very briefly with sauce. Transfer meat to a warm serving platter; spoon sauce over veal and serve on a bed of rice.

"This is my dad's favorite dish. I make this for him every year on his birthday."

Linda Brayton   **Grace Davis High School, Modesto, CA**

WISCONSIN PASTA PIZZA

Serves 8   *Photo opposite page 96*

2 cups corkscrew macaroni, uncooked
3 eggs, beaten
½ cup milk
½ cup Wisconsin Cheddar cheese, shredded
¼ cup onion, finely chopped
1 pound lean ground beef
1 (15 ounce) can tomato sauce
1 teaspoon dried basil, crushed
1 teaspoon dried oregano, crushed
½ teaspoon garlic salt
1 (medium) tomato, thinly sliced
1 green pepper, sliced into rings
2 cups Wisconsin Mozzarella cheese, shredded

Cook macaroni according to package directions; drain well. Combine eggs and milk; stir into cooked macaroni. Stir in cheddar cheese and onion; mix well. Spread macaroni mixture evenly over a well-buttered 14" pizza pan. Bake at 350 degrees for 25 minutes. Meanwhile, in large skillet, cook ground beef until browned; drain excess fat. Stir in tomato sauce, basil, oregano and garlic salt. Spoon meat mixture over baked macaroni crust. Arrange tomato slices and pepper rings over meat mixture. Sprinkle with mozzarella cheese. Bake about 15 minutes or until cheese is bubbly.

Wisconsin Milk Marketing Board, Inc.   **Madison, WI**

ZUCCHINI LASAGNA

Serves 4 - 5

3 tablespoons onion, chopped
1 tablespoon oil
½ pound ground beef
1 (8 ounce) can tomato sauce
¼ teaspoon garlic salt
¼ teaspoon dried oregano
¼ teaspoon dried basil
dash pepper
1 egg, slightly beaten
½ cup cottage cheese
2 (medium) zucchini, sliced lengthwise into ¼" thick slices
1 tablespoon all-purpose flour
¼ pound mozzarella cheese, shredded
2 tablespoons Parmesan cheese, grated

Saute onion in oil until tender. Add ground beef and cook until no longer pink; drain excess fat. Add tomato sauce, garlic salt, oregano, basil and pepper. Simmer, covered, 10 minutes. Mix egg and cottage cheese together; set aside. In bottom of casserole dish, arrange a layer of zucchini and sprinkle with ½ tablespoon flour. Top with all the cottage cheese mixture, then one half of the mozzarella and Parmesan cheeses, and one half of the meat mixture. Repeat with remaining zucchini; sprinkle with flour; layer remaining cheese and top with meat mixture. Bake, uncovered, at 375 degrees for 40 minutes or until hot and bubbly and zucchini is fork tender. Let stand 5 to 10 minutes before cutting.

"This is a nice change from traditional lasagna and easier to make since there aren't any noodles to cook."

Jan Neufeld   **Fullerton High School, Fullerton, CA**

ZUCCHINI LASAGNA (NO NOODLES)
Serves 6 - 8

- 8 ounces cream cheese
- 1 cup cottage cheese
- 1 cup sour cream
- $\frac{1}{4}$ cup green onion, chopped
- $\frac{1}{4}$ cup green pepper, chopped
- 1 $\frac{1}{2}$ pounds ground beef
- $\frac{1}{2}$ teaspoon oregano
- $\frac{1}{2}$ teaspoon basil
- $\frac{1}{2}$ teaspoon rosemary
- $\frac{1}{2}$ teaspoon salt
- 1 can tomato sauce
- 2 $\frac{1}{2}$ pounds zucchini, thinly sliced

In a bowl, combine cream cheese with cottage cheese, sour cream, onion and green pepper. Brown ground beef with seasonings; stir in tomato sauce. In a 9" x 12" greased casserole, thinly layer a small amount of meat mixture; make a layer of zucchini, cover with layer of cheese mixture. Repeat until all ingredients are used, ending with the meat mixture. Cover and bake at 350 degrees for 30 minutes. Uncover and bake 30 minutes more.

Karyn Hobbs   **Lemoore High School, Lemoore, CA**

Rinse pasta using a small amount of cold tap water to stop the cooking process. Be sure not to use so much that it cools off the pasta, if serving hot.

Nancy Murray   **El Capitan HS, Lakeside, CA**

ASPARAGUS & BACON PASTA

Serves 6

1 pound penne pasta
12 ounces bacon, thickly sliced
1 1/4 pound (medium) asparagus, cut into 1" pieces
1/8 teaspoon red pepper flakes
2 tablespoons fresh marjoram leaves
12 ounces mozzarella cheese, cut into 1/2" cubes
salt and freshly ground pepper, to taste

Bring large pot of salted water to a boil. Add pasta and cook 5 to 7 minutes; drain and set aside. Cook bacon until crisp; drain, crumble and set aside. Discard all but 1/4 cup bacon fat and return to pan. Add asparagus, red pepper flakes and marjoram. Cook until asparagus is lightly browned. Add pasta, crumbled bacon and salt and pepper to pan. Toss until combined. Add mozzarella and toss again. Serve.

"Wonderful entree or use as a side dish. Great and unusual flavor."

Robin Ali　　　　　　　　**Nevada Union High School, Grass Valley, CA**

EASY ITALIAN SAUSAGE SANDWICH

Serves 4 - 6

6 links Italian sausage, hot or mild
6 to 12 thin slices mozzarella cheese
6 Italian style sandwich rolls (hoagie style)
1 (small) can tomato sauce
garlic salt and pepper, to taste
Parmesan cheese, grated, to taste

Simmer sausage in a covered fry pan with just enough water to cover bottom of pan. Cook on medium-high until water is gone. Remove lid and continue to cook until sausage is lightly browned. Remove from heat and slice each sausage lengthwise. Place cheese on inside of sausage and cook over low heat until cheese melts. Split rolls in half and spread with mixture of warm tomato sauce, garlic salt and pepper. Place sausage on one half of roll. Top sausage with extra sauce and Parmesan cheese, if desired. Place the other half of roll on top and enjoy.

"Serve with your favorite salad or side dish. Great for a hot lunch or dinner.
This is a quick and easy, long time favorite of my family."

Georgette Phillips　　　　　　**Silverado High School, Victorville, CA**

EGG ROLL CANNELONI
Serves 6

Sausage filling:
8 ounces mild Italian sausages
1 (10 ounce) package frozen chopped spinach
2 cups ricotta cheese
2 egg yolks
1 cup Parmesan cheese, grated
$\frac{1}{8}$ teaspoon pepper
$\frac{3}{4}$ teaspoon oregano
Sauce:
3 tablespoons olive oil
2 onions, chopped
2 cloves garlic, minced
1 (28 ounce) can Italian tomatoes, diced
1 $\frac{1}{2}$ teaspoons dried mint
1 $\frac{1}{2}$ teaspoons dried basil
1 cup chicken broth
$\frac{1}{2}$ cup whipping cream
salt and pepper to taste
12 egg roll skins
1 pound jack cheese, shredded

Filling: Remove casings from sausages. Fry until browned; drain excess fat. Squeeze liquid from frozen spinach and combine with sausage, ricotta, egg yolks, Parmesan, pepper and oregano.

Sauce: In a large frying pan, saute onion and garlic in olive oil. Add tomatoes, mint, basil and broth. Simmer, uncovered, until sauce is reduced to 6 cups, about 20 minutes. Stir in whipping cream. Salt and pepper to taste.

Preheat oven to 400 degrees. Mound $\frac{1}{3}$ cup filling along one edge of each egg roll skin. Roll to close. Spread half of the sauce in a 9" x 13" baking dish. Place egg roll "canneloni" seam side down. Spread with remaining sauce. Top each with slice of cheese. Bake, uncovered, 30 to 40 minutes.

"This takes a little time, but tastes wonderful. I usually make this a day ahead so we can spend the day skiing. When we come home, I just stick this in the oven and dinner is ready!

Kris Hawkins   **Clovis West High School, Fresno, CA**

FESTIVE LASAGNA
Serves 12

$\frac{1}{2}$ of a (1 pound) package lasagna, uncooked
2 pounds bulk Italian sausage
1 (medium) onion, chopped
2 cloves garlic, minced
1 (28 ounce) can whole tomatoes, cut up, undrained
1 (12 ounce) can tomato paste
2 teaspoons sugar
3 teaspoons salt, divided
1 $\frac{1}{2}$ teaspoons basil leaves
1 teaspoon crushed red pepper
$\frac{1}{4}$ teaspoon pepper
2 (15 ounce) containers ricotta cheese
1 egg, beaten
$\frac{1}{3}$ cup fresh parsley, chopped
4 cups mozzarella cheese, shredded
1 cup Parmesan cheese, grated

Prepare lasagna according to package directions; drain. In Dutch oven, combine sausage, onion and garlic. Cook until sausage is no longer pink, stirring occasionally; drain excess fat. Stir in tomatoes, tomato paste, sugar, 2 teaspoons salt, basil, red pepper and pepper; bring to a boil. Reduce heat and simmer 20 minutes. In medium bowl, blend ricotta, egg, parsley and 1 teaspoon salt. Spread a thin layer of sauce in 9" x 13" baking pan. Layer one third each lasagna, remaining sauce, ricotta mixture, mozzarella and Parmesan cheeses. Repeat layers. Bake at 375 degrees until bubbly, about 1 hour. Let stand 5 minutes before cutting.

April Berry   **Temecula Valley High School, Temecula, CA**

FETTUCCINI WITH MINT, PEAS & HAM
Serves 4

2 tablespoons olive oil
2 leeks, white part only, diced
2 cloves garlic, minced
1 cup chicken broth
2 tablespoons flour
1 cup half & half
3 ounces ham, cooked, cut into $\frac{1}{4}$" strips
1 cup peas, frozen
salt and pepper, to taste
1 pound fettuccini, fresh
$\frac{1}{2}$ cup mint, fresh, chopped

Heat olive oil in skillet over medium heat; saute leeks with garlic until soft. Add chicken broth. Stir flour into half & half, then add to skillet, stirring until thickened. Add ham and peas. Season to taste with salt and pepper. Cook fettuccini in rapidly boiling water for approximately 6 to 8 minutes, until tender; drain. Toss fettuccini with sauce and sprinkle with mint.

Anne Silveira   **Shasta High School, Redding, CA**

Italian Sausage & Peppers
Serves 4

3 green peppers, stemmed, seeded, cut into chunks
3 tablespoons olive oil
salt and pepper, to taste
1 pound Italian sausages
¾ cup red wine

In oven proof pan, saute green peppers in oil until they are softened. Season with salt and pepper, to taste. Remove peppers from pan and set aside. Brown sausages in same pan. When browned, add wine. Return peppers to pan. Cover with foil and bake at 350 degrees for 40 minutes. Uncover peppers and bake another 30 minutes.

"This was adapted from an old Frank Sinatra/Dinah Shore recipe.
Serve with rice, crusty garlic bread and a green salad."

Margaret McLeod   **Nogales High School, La Puente, CA**

Lasagna
Serves 6

1 pound hot Italian sausage
1 clove garlic, minced
1 tablespoon basil
1 ½ teaspoon salt
1 (16 ounce) can tomatoes
1 (12 ounce) can tomato paste
16 ounces lasagna noodles
3 cups cottage cheese
½ cup Parmesan cheese, grated
2 tablespoons parsley flakes
2 eggs, beaten
2 teaspoons salt
½ teaspoon pepper
1 pound mozzarella cheese, shredded

Brown sausage; drain excess fat. Add next five ingredients and simmer, uncovered, 30 minutes. Meanwhile, cook noodles according to package directions; drain. Combine cottage cheese, Parmesan, parsley, eggs, salt and pepper. In baking dish, layer half of the noodles, cheese mixture, mozzarella and meat sauce; repeat. Bake at 375 degrees for 30 minutes.

"Add a tossed salad and garlic bread, You're ready for some fine dining!"

Debbie Rothe   **Alta Loma High School, Alta Loma, CA**

Lemon Ravioli
Serves 4 - 5

1 pound ravioli, fresh or frozen
1 pound asparagus, cut into 1 ½" pieces
½ cup margarine
1 cup half & half
1 tablespoon lemon peel, grated
½ cup Parmesan cheese, grated
1 cup cooked ham, diced

Cook ravioli as directed on label; with 3 minutes left to cook, add asparagus pieces to

Pasta Pizza
Pizza or pasta? Have both!
(page 91)

Margherite Pizza
Mozarella, roma tomatoes
and fresh basil. (page 52)

Veal Piccata
A classic favorite.
(page 90)

water. Cook and drain. Place in large serving bowl. In a small saucepan, heat margarine, half & half and lemon peel for 5 minutes over medium heat. Stir in cheese and ham. Pour sauce over ravioli and toss to coat.

"When fresh asparagus appears at Farmer's Market, I pull out this recipe."
Sue Waterbury   **San Luis Obispo High School, San Luis Obispo, CA**

MACARONI & CHEESE DELUXE
Serves 4 - 6

    1 ½ cups elbow macaroni
    5 tablespoons butter, divided
    4 tablespoons flour
    2 cups milk
    1 cup Velveeta cheese, cubed
    ½ teaspoon salt
    2 links Italian sausage
    1 green onion, chopped
    1 cup cheddar cheese, grated
    2 slices bread
    garlic salt, to taste

Cook macaroni according to package directions; drain. In saucepan, melt 4 tablespoons butter. Add flour; cook and stir 2 minutes. Add milk, stirring constantly until thickened. Add cheese cubes to sauce and stir until melted. Season to taste with salt. While sauce is cooking, crumble sausage and saute until cooked. In a casserole dish, place half of the macaroni; pour half of the cheese sauce over. Layer sausage on top with green onions. Repeat with macaroni and sauce. Sprinkle cheddar cheese over top. Butter bread slices, sprinkle with garlic salt and cut into cubes. Sprinkle on top of casserole. Bake at 350 degrees for 20 to 30 minutes, until cheese melts and croutons brown.

"I borrowed this recipe from George Yackey at Santana High School 10 years ago and my students agree that it's the best! We make it and enjoy it in one 90 minute class period."
Beth Leighton   **Helix High School, La Mesa, CA**

MAFALDA WITH SAUSAGE & MUSHROOMS
Serves 6 - 8

    12 ounces bulk sweet Italian sausage
    2 cups fresh cremini and/or button mushrooms
    1 (28 ounce) can crushed tomatoes
    1 (8 ounce) can tomato sauce
    1 (6 ounce) can tomato paste
    ⅔ cup water
    1 (medium) onion, chopped
    1 tablespoon sugar
    1 teaspoon dried rosemary OR 1 tablespoon fresh
    ¼ teaspoon pepper
    2 cloves garlic, minced
    9 to 12 ounces dried mafalda or other pasta
    Garnish: Freshly grated Parmesan cheese

In large skillet, brown sausage; drain excess fat. In a 3 to 4 quart crockery cooker, combine mushrooms, tomatoes, tomato sauce, tomato paste, water, onion, sugar, rosemary, pepper and garlic. Stir in sausage. Cover; cook on low heat for 6 to 8 hours or on high heat setting for 3 to 4 hours. Just before serving, cook pasta according to package directions; drain. Serve sausage mixture over pastas. If desired, sprinkle with Parmesan cheese.

"This has a surprisingly low 358 calories per serving and only 10 grams of fat. Enjoy! Mafalda is a long narrow or medium-width noodle with ruffled edges and resembles a lasagna noodle. If you can't find it, use fettuccini or spaghetti instead."

Pam Ford   **Temecula Valley High School, Temecula, CA**

NINE LAYER DINNER
Serves 8

8 ounces rotelle
8 ounces Swiss cheese, shredded
3/4 pound cooked ham, diced
1 (10 ounce) package frozen peas
1 (16 ounce) can tomatoes, diced
1 (12 ounce) can whole kernel corn
2 ounces pimiento, diced
1 (10.75 ounce) can cream of celery soup
1/2 cup milk or half & half
1 cup soft bread crumbs

Cook rotelle according to package directions; drain. Place cooked rotelli in greased 9" x 13" baking dish. Cover with Swiss cheese, ham and peas. Place layer of tomatoes, corn and pimiento. Thin the soup with milk or half & half. Pour over casserole. Spread soft bread crumbs over top. Bake at 350 degrees for 40 minutes.

Mary Lash   **Paramount High School, Paramount, CA**

PEPPERONI PIZZA CASSEROLE
Serves 8

8 lasagna noodles
1/2 pound bulk Italian sausage
2 cups mozzarella cheese, shredded, divided
1/2 cup Parmesan cheese, grated
1/2 teaspoon oregano
8 ounces pizza sauce
4 ounces pepperoni, sliced
1 (small) green pepper, sliced
1 (small) jar mushrooms, sliced

Cook lasagna noodles according to package directions; drain. Cook sausage and drain excess fat. Arrange half of the noodles in an ungreased 13" x 9" x 2" pan. Sprinkle 3/4 cup mozzarella, 1/4 cup Parmesan cheese and oregano over noodles. Top with remaining noodles. Spoon pizza sauce over noodles. Arrange sausage, pepperoni, peppers and mushrooms on top. Bake at 350 degrees 15 minutes. Sprinkle on remaining cheese and bake 15 minutes more. Cut into squares to serve.

"This recipe was given to me by Mary Alice Moyer, an English teacher at Huntington Beach High School. It's excellent!"

Marie Coots   **Huntington Beach High School, Huntington Beach, CA**

PEPPY PIZZA PASTA

Serves 8

7 ounces elbow macaroni, cooked
1 pound ground Italian sausage
1 cup onion, chopped
3.5 ounces or 1 cup pepperoni, chopped
15 ounces pizza sauce
8 ounces tomato sauce
4 ounces mushrooms, sliced
2 1/3 ounces olives, sliced, drained
8 ounces mozzarella cheese, shredded

Prepare macaroni according to package directions. Brown sausage with onion; drain excess fat. In a bowl, combine all ingredients, except cheese and pour into a 13" x 9" baking pan. Sprinkle cheese over top. Cover an bake at 350 degrees for 45 minutes. Uncover and bake 5 to 10 minutes more, or until cheese is melted.

"I served this for dinner while the eight of us cruised in a Duffy boat and watched the Balboa Boat Parade. They all enjoyed it!"

Gail Hurt Knieriem   **Estancia High School, Costa Mesa, CA**

PIZZA QUICHE

Serves 6 - 8

4 ounces Italian sausage, cooked
Pastry for double crust pie
1 cup ricotta cheese
4 eggs, divided
1 cup mozzarella cheese, shredded
1/2 cup pepperoni, chopped
1/2 cup prosciutto or ham, cubed
1/2 cup salami, cut into strips
1/4 cup Parmesan cheese, grated
2 tablespoon milk

Brown sausage; drain excess fat. Line a 9" pie pan with crust; crimp edges. Do not prick! Bake 4 to 5 minutes in 450 degree oven. Remove. Reduce oven temperature to 350 degrees. Beat together ricotta and 3 eggs; fold in sausage, mozzarella, pepperoni, prosciutto or ham, salami and Parmesan. Turn into partially baked pastry shell. Roll out remaining pastry to 8" circle. Cut into 6 to 8 wedges and place on top of filling. Bake 20 minutes. Combine remaining egg and milk; brush pastry wedges. Continue baking 20 minutes more, until golden brown. Allow to cool 10 minutes before serving.

"This is a favorite of my special friend, Louise Geracci."

Mary M. Rector   **Valley High School, Las Vegas, NV**

RIGATONI
Serves 6

    1 box rigatoni
    1 pound sweet Italian sausage
    4 tablespoons olive oil
    ½ cup black olives, chopped
    ½ cup pimiento, in water, drained
    ⅓ cup parsley, chopped
    8 to 10 large fresh basil leaves, or 1 teaspoon dried
    2 to 3 cloves garlic, peeled, minced
    2 cups Parmesan cheese, grated
    salt and pepper, to taste

Cook pasta according to package directions, drain. While pasta cooks, brown sausage in skillet. Slice sausage and keep warm. In an soup pot, heat olive oil; stir in olives, pimiento, parsley, basil and garlic, Stir 1 minute, then add cooked pasta and sliced sausage. Add Parmesan cheese and toss gently so pasta does not break apart. Season with salt and pepper, to taste. NOTE: Shrimp may be substituted for sausage.

Jill Marsh   **Warren High School, Downey, CA**

SPAGHETTI ALLA CARBONARA
Serves 4

    6 slices bacon, cooked, chopped
    8 ounces thin pasta
    1 egg, beaten
    ¼ cup butter, melted
    2 tablespoons olive oil, divided
    1 tablespoon fresh parsley, chopped
    2 tablespoons fresh chives, chopped
    ¼ cup dry white vermouth
    salt and pepper, to taste
    ¾ cup Parmesan cheese, freshly grated
    ¼ cup cream or half & half

Fry bacon until crisp; drain on paper towel and set aside. Cook and drain pasta according to package directions. Place in large bowl. Beat egg, then toss with pasta, butter and 1 tablespoon olive oil. Saute parsley, chives and vermouth in 1 tablespoon olive oil for 5 minutes. Toss in bacon pieces, reserving some for topping. While tossing, sprinkle with salt and pepper, Parmesan and ⅛ cup of the cream or half & half. Continue tossing until mixture is smooth and flavored to your satisfaction. If necessary, add more cream or half & half. Garnish with remaining bacon pieces.

"Have all ingredients prepared and ready to toss into pasta so it can be served warm."

Pat Johnson   **Iron Horse Middle School, San Ramon, CA**

SPAGHETTI BAKE
Serves 4 - 6

- 1 (8 ounce) package spaghetti
- 1 egg, beaten
- 2 cups mozzarella cheese, shredded, divided
- 1/4 cup Parmesan cheese, grated
- nonstick cooking spray
- 1/2 pound ground beef
- 1/2 pound Italian sausage, casings removed, crumbled
- 1 3/4 cup spaghetti sauce

Cook spaghetti according to package directions. Rinse with cold water and drain.Toss with beaten egg, 1 cup mozzarella and Parmesan cheese. Lightly spray an 8" x 10" baking dish with nonstick cooking spray. Place spaghetti mixture in dish. Meanwhile, brown ground beef and sausage in medium skillet on medium heat; drain excess fat. Stir in spaghetti sauce. Cook on low heat 5 minutes. Spoon meat sauce over spaghetti and top with remaining cheeses. Bake at 375 degrees for 15 minutes. Let stand 5 minutes before serving.

Sally Engel   **Elsinore Middle School, Lake Elsinore, CA**

SPAGHETTI PIE
Serves 8

- 8 ounces thin spaghetti
- 2 eggs
- 1/4 cup Parmesan cheese, grated
- 1/2 cup green pepper, chopped
- 1/3 cup onion, chopped
- 2 tablespoons butter
- 1 cup sour cream
- 1 pound hot or sweet Italian sausage, casings removed
- 1 cup water
- 1 (6 ounce) can tomato paste
- 4 to 8 ounces mozzarella cheese, grated

Break spaghetti in half and cook according to package directions; drain. In medium bowl, beat eggs and Parmesan cheese. Add warm, drained spaghetti and toss to mix. Line a greased 10" pie pan with spaghetti mixture, forming a crust; set aside. In large skillet, saute green pepper and onion in butter for 5 minutes. Stir in sour cream; spoon over spaghetti crust. In 3 quart saucepan over medium heat, cook sausage until no longer pink, breaking it up with spoon as it cooks. Drain off excess fat. Add water and tomato paste to sausage, mixing well. Heat to boiling. Reduce heat and simmer, uncovered 10 minutes, until slightly thickened, stirring once or twice. Spoon over sour cream mixture. Cover pie with foil and bake in a preheated 350 degree oven for 25 minutes. Remove foil and sprinkle mozzarella cheese over sausage mix. Bake 3 to 5 minutes more, until cheese melts. Let stand 5 minutes before cutting.

"This recipe was given to me by a colleague and friend, Lynn Valdez.
Everyone who samples it asks for the recipe. Delicious!"

Vicki Pearl   **Giano Intermediate School, La Puente, CA**

SPECIAL SAUCE RIGATONI
Serves 4

> 2 tablespoons butter
> 1 small onion, chopped
> 2 cloves garlic, minced
> 1 tablespoon dried Italian seasoning
> 1 (16 ounce) can Italian plum tomatoes, chopped (reserve juice)
> 3 ounces prosciutto or ham, sliced, chopped
> 1/2 cup vodka
> 3/4 cup whipping cream
> 1 cup Parmesan cheese, grated, divided
> 8 ounces rigatoni or other pasta, freshly cooked

Melt butter in heavy skillet over medium-high heat. Add onion, garlic and Italian seasoning and saute until onion is translucent, about 4 minutes. Add tomatoes, reserved juice and proscuitto or ham; simmer 10 minutes, stirring occasionally. Add vodka and simmer 5 minutes. Stir in cream and 1/2 cup Parmesan. Simmer until sauce slightly thickens, about 4 minutes. Toss hot cooked pasta with sauce until well coated. Season with salt and pepper. Serve, passing remaining 1/2 cup Parmesan cheese.

"My friend, Marie Harlan, is one of the best cooks I know. We met in our college Foods & Nutrition class about 30 years ago. This recipe is one of her favorites - and mine!"
Kathy Warren   **C.K. McClatchy High School, Sacramento, CA**

THE ITALIAN SCRAMBLE
Serves 4 - 6

> 1 tablespoon olive oil
> 1 medium potato, cubed
> 1/2 pound sweet Italian sausages
> 1 (small) onion, chopped
> 1 (small) green pepper, chopped
> 1 (small) red pepper, chopped
> 8 eggs
> 2 tablespoons milk
> 1/8 teaspoon oregano
> 1 firm, ripe tomato, seeded, chopped
> 1/2 cup mozzarella cheese, shredded
> 1/4 cup Parmesan cheese, grated

Heat olive oil in large frying pan and add potato. Cook over medium heat, stirring occasionally. Remove sausage casings and crumble meat into frying pan, cooking and stirring until lightly browned. Add onions and peppers and cook until onion is limp and potato cubes are done. Beat eggs with milk and oregano. All at once, add tomatoes, egg mixture and mozzarella into frying pan. Lower heat and cook, stirring lightly until eggs are soft and fluffy, not hard and stiff. Top with grated cheese and serve.

"I have omitted the eggs and used the mixture on rigatoni topped with Alfredo sauce. Top with chopped, fresh parsley and serve with hot Italian bread."
Millie Deeton   **Ayala High School, Chino Hills, CA**

BASIL-SCALLOP LINGUINE

Serves 6

1 tablespoon olive oil
2 (medium) cloves garlic, crushed
2 shallots, minced
2 tablespoons fresh basil, minced
2 tablespoons Italian parsley, minced
3 teaspoons salt, divided
$\frac{1}{4}$ teaspoon red pepper flakes
$\frac{1}{4}$ teaspoon ground black pepper
1 (16 ounce) can whole tomatoes
$\frac{1}{2}$ cup dry white wine
2 tablespoons tomato paste
3 quarts water
1 tablespoon vegetable oil
1 (8 ounce) package linguine
1 pound sea scallops
1 (9 ounce) package frozen artichoke hearts, thawed
2 tablespoons pine nuts
Garnish: Italian parsley

In a 3 quart saucepan over medium heat, heat olive oil. When hot, add garlic and shallots. Cook, stirring constantly with a wooden spoon, until tender but not brown. Remove from heat. Add basil, parsley, 1 teaspoon salt, red pepper flakes, black pepper, tomatoes, wine and tomato paste in saucepan. Return to heat and bring to a boil, stirring to break up tomatoes. Cover, reduce heat and simmer 20 minutes. In a 4 quart saucepan, bring water, 2 teaspoons salt and vegetable oil to a rolling boil. Add linguine, stirring to separate strands. Cover until water returns to boiling. Uncover and cook 8 to 10 minutes or until tender. While linguine cooks, place scallops in a colander. Rinse under cold water; drain thoroughly. Cut each scallop in half and add to tomato mixture along with artichoke hearts. Cook 5 minutes or until scallops are tender and artichokes are hot; set aside. Place pine nuts in small skillet over moderately high heat. (It's not necessary to add oil to the skillet.) Cook, stirring constantly, until pine nuts turn light golden brown. Remove from heat and set aside. Drain cooked linguine. Place on a large serving platter. Spoon tomato mixture over pasta. Toss gently until thoroughly combined. Sprinkle with toasted pine nuts and garnish with fresh Italian parsley.

"Delicious, easy and workable for large groups!"

Debra Purcell   **Cope Middle School, Redlands, CA**

CALISTOGA INN FETTUCCINI & SALMON
Serves 4

1 pound fettuccini, cooked, drained
4 cups whipping cream
½ cup butter
8 to 12 ounces smoked salmon, julienned
¼ cup fresh chives, minced
freshly ground pepper, to taste
Garnish: Fresh parsley or tarragon

Prepare fettuccini according to package directions; drain. Combine whipping cream and butter in medium saucepan and cook over medium high heat until thick, glossy and reduced by half. Add salmon, chives and pepper. Cook, stirring gently, about 1 minute. Pour sauce over hot, cooked fettuccini. Garnish with parsley or tarragon.

Cindy Johnson   **Orland High School, Orland, CA**

GRILLED TUNA PASTA TOSS
Serves 4

1 pound fresh tuna steak
1 teaspoon seasoning salt, divided
1 teaspoon dried sweet basil, divided
½ package angel hair pasta
2 tablespoons olive oil
1 teaspoon garlic minced
½ (large) white onion
1 quart fresh spinach
¼ cup sun-dried tomatoes, diced (optional)
2 tablespoons capers

Lightly season tuna steak with ½ teaspoon seasoning salt and ½ teaspoon basil. Grill or broil, being careful not to overcook. After cooking, cool, then flake into small pieces; set aside. Cook pasta according to package directions. In a large frying pan, heat olive oil and quickly saute garlic with remaining ½ teaspoon seasoning salt. When garlic just starts to brown, add onion, remaining ½ teaspoon basil, spinach and sun-dried tomatoes (if using). Continue cooking until onion and spinach are done, 3 to 5 minutes on medium-high heat. Lower heat. Add cooked and drained pasta, tuna and capers; toss well.

Karen Peters   **Vaca Peña Middle School, Vacaville, CA**

LINGUINE WITH SCALLOPS
Serves 4

1 pound fresh bay scallops
juice of ½ lemon
1 bunch Italian parsley
1 clove garlic, minced
pinch nutmeg, freshly grated
salt and freshly ground pepper, to taste
5 tablespoons butter
⅓ cup heavy cream
1 pound linguine, cooked, drained
Garnish: Parmesan cheese, freshly grated

Wash scallops under cold water; drain and place in bowl with lemon juice. In another bowl, combine parsley, garlic, nutmeg, salt and pepper. Add scallops and marinate 10 minutes. Heat butter in skillet. Add scallops and marinade to butter and saute 3 to 4 minutes. Add cream and reduce 1 minute. Adjust seasonings. Serve over cooked linguine. Top with freshly grated Parmesan cheese.

Nancy Hunyadi　　　　　　　　　**Fullerton High School, Fullerton, CA**

LOWFAT FETTUCCINI ALFREDO
Serves 4
- 1 package fettuccini
- 2 tablespoons butter
- 2 tablespoons flour
- 2 cups nonfat milk
- 1/4 teaspoon salt
- 1/4 teaspoon pepper
- 1/2 cup Parmesan cheese, grated
- 1/2 pound shrimp, cooked

Cook fettuccini according to package directions. Melt butter in medium saucepan. Stir in flour to form a roux (let it bubble). Add milk, all at once. Stir frequently until sauce simmers. Do not boil. Add salt, pepper and Parmesan cheese. Add cooked shrimp and heat through. Drain fettuccini and serve with sauce.

"My husband enjoys Fettuccini Alfredo but it's too high in fat... he loves this dish!"

Elizabeth Thornburg　　　　　　**Selma High School, Selma, CA**

MR. GOLD'S SHRIMP SCAMPI LINGUINE
Serves 4
- 8 ounces linguine
- 4 cloves garlic, minced
- 2 tablespoons olive oil
- 8 tablespoons butter
- 8 ounces (medium to large size) shrimp, peeled, deveined
- 1 whole lemon, juiced
- 4 tablespoons parsley, minced
- dash salt and white pepper
- 1/4 cup white wine (non alcoholic works well also)
- 2 tablespoons Italian seasoned bread crumbs

Cook linguine according to package directions. Do not overcook. Drain but do not rinse. In large skillet, lightly saute minced garlic in olive oil. Add butter and heat until it foams. Add shrimp and saute. Add lemon juice and parsley. Salt and pepper, to taste. Add wine and cook one minute. Sprinkle with bread crumbs one tablespoon at a time and stir. The bread crumbs thicken the sauce so you should be careful not to add too much. Turn off heat immediately; stir gently. Place drained, hot linguine in serving dishes. Spoon scampi sauce with shrimp over pasta. Serve immediately.

"Mr. Gold, who is one of our Assistant Principals, demonstrates this recipe each year. My catering students love it!"

Sandy Hughes　　　　　　　　　**Upland High School, Upland, CA**

PASTA WITH GARLIC & CLAMS
Serves 4

3 tablespoons butter
3 tablespoons oil
2 cloves garlic, minced
1 3/4 cups bottled clam juice
1/3 cup white wine or chicken broth
1 1/2 teaspoons dried oregano leaves
1/4 teaspoon crushed red pepper flakes
1 (12 ounce) package pasta
1/2 cup parsley, chopped
2 cans clams, chopped

In large skillet, heat butter and oil. Add garlic and cook 1 minute. Add clam juice, wine or chicken broth, oregano and red pepper. Boil, uncovered until liquid is reduced by half; about 10 minutes. Cook pasta according to package directions; drain. Add parsley and clams to sauce; pour over pasta and toss.

"I use angel hair pasta. I love the flavor of this dish."

Pat Hufnagel   **Esperanza High School, Anaheim, CA**

SCALLOPS & SHRIMP WITH LINGUINE
Serves 4

1 pound prawns, shelled, cleaned
1 pound scallops
1/2 cup butter
2 to 3 cloves garlic minced
1 cup white wine
1 pound linguine, boiled, lightly buttered

Shell, clean and rinse prawns and scallops. Melt butter in heavy saucepan. Saute prawns, scallops and garlic. When prawns are almost completely pink and scallops are white, add white wine and finish cooking. Meanwhile, cook linguine according to package directions; drain and lightly toss with butter. Serve seafood over pasta.

"Serve with a salad and French bread. It brings everyone home for dinner!"

Gail McAuley   **Lincoln High School, Stockton, CA**

SPAGHETTI WITH WHITE CLAM SAUCE
Serves 6

1/2 cup butter
1 onion, chopped
2 cloves garlic, minced
1/3 cup flour
2 cups milk
2 (6.5 ounce) cans clams, minced
1/2 teaspoon basil leaves
1/2 teaspoon salt
1/8 teaspoon white pepper
2 tablespoons fresh parsley, minced
1 (12 ounce) package spaghetti, cooked and drained

Melt butter in medium saucepan; add onion and garlic and saute until tender. Stir in flour. Slowly add milk, stirring constantly until sauce thickens. Drain clams,

reserving juice. Add clam juice to sauce. Stir in basil, salt, pepper and parsley. Simmer about 15 minutes. Prepare spaghetti according to package directions; drain. Add clams to sauce and warm through. Spoon clam sauce over hot, cooked spaghetti.
"Delicious and easy! Prepare sauce in an electric fry pan - easy clean up!"
Patsy Graves   **Bingham High School, So. Jordan, UT**

STUFFED MANICOTTI & CRABMEAT SAUCE
Serves 4
   8 ounces fresh or frozen crabmeat
   1 cup onion, chopped
   1 clove garlic, minced
   2 tablespoons cooking oil
   1 (1 pound) can tomatoes
   1 (8 ounce) can tomato sauce
   1 teaspoon basil
   1 teaspoon salt, divided
   8 manicotti noodles
   1 ½ cups cottage cheese
   ¾ cup Parmesan cheese, shredded
   1 egg, beaten
   2 tablespoons parsley, chopped

Drain and flake crabmeat; set aside. Cook onion and garlic in oil until onion is limp. Add tomatoes, tomato sauce, basil and ½ teaspoon salt. Bring to a simmer and cook 25 to 30 minutes, uncovered. Stir in crabmeat. Spread ⅓ of the sauce over bottom of a shallow 1 ½ quart casserole. While sauce is cooking, cook manicotti as directed on package; drain and rinse in cold water. Combine and mix cottage cheese, ½ cup Parmesan cheese, egg, parsley and remaining ½ teaspoon salt. Fill noodles with cheese mixture and arrange on sauce in casserole. Spoon remaining sauce over filled noodles. Cover dish with foil and bake at 350 degrees for 25 minutes. Uncover and bake 15 to 20 minutes longer. Sprinkle with remaining ¼ cup Parmesan cheese over top when done.
Joanne Montoy   **Esperanza High School, Anaheim, CA**

TAGLIATELLE, SCALLOPS & SALMON
Serves 4
   3 tablespoons unsalted butter
   1 clove garlic, crushed
   1 tablespoon onion, grated
   16 (small) scallops, cleaned and soaked in milk for 30 minutes
   1 pound fresh tagliatelle or ¾ pound dried
   ⅔ cup dry white wine
   2 teaspoons fresh parsley, finely chopped
   salt and pepper, to taste
   ⅔ cup cream
   4 ounces smoked salmon, julienned

Heat butter and gently saute garlic and onion for 1 to 2 minutes. Add drained scallops and quickly fry until opaque. Put tagliatelle on to cook in boiling, salted water. Add wine and parsley to scallops and heat over high heat until liquid is reduced by half. Season to taste with salt and pepper. Stir in cream. Lower heat and cook until cream begins to thicken. Drain tagliatelle when al dente and transfer to a

warm serving dish. Pour on sauce, add salmon and toss quickly before serving.
Peggy Herndon   **Central Valley High School, Shasta Lake City, CA**

TROUT WITH PROSCIUTTO
Serves 6

3 tablespoons olive oil, divided
6 whole trout
6 tablespoons soft bread crumbs
3 cloves garlic, chopped
2 tablespoons parsley, chopped
6 tablespoons prosciutto, chopped
freshly ground pepper
lemon wedges

Preheat oven to 475 degrees. Slash trout diagonally 2 times on each side, about 1/4"
to 1/2" deep. Use 2 tablespoons olive oil to brush each fillet, on both sides. Mix
together bread crumbs, garlic, parsley, prosciutto and remaining 1 tablespoon olive
oil. Lightly fill slashes with mixture. Sprinkle with freshly ground pepper and place
on baking sheet. Bake 12 to 15 minutes. Serve with lemon wedges.

"You may use boneless trout. Spread 2 tablespoons bread crumbs in cavity."
Martha Goodwin   **Golden Valley High School, Merced, CA**

ARMIDA'S LINGUINE
Serves 4

1 package linguine, cooked
1/2 onion, finely chopped
1 to 2 tablespoons olive oil
2 to 3 cloves garlic, minced
1 cup fresh mushrooms, sliced
2 carrots, peeled, sliced
2 zucchini, sliced, cut in halves
2 cans Italian style stewed tomatoes
2 tablespoons tomato paste (Italian seasoned)
salt, to taste
pepper, freshly ground, to taste
1/4 cup fresh basil leaves, chopped
Garnish: Parmesan cheese, grated

Prepare linguine according to package directions. Saute onion in olive oil 2 to 3
minutes in a large skillet. Add garlic and mushrooms, continue to saute. Add carrots
and saute 1 to 2 minutes before adding zucchini. Add tomatoes and tomato paste,
stirring all ingredients together well. Season with salt and pepper, to taste. When all
ingredients are simmering, add basil. Serve over prepared linguine and sprinkle
with Parmesan cheese.

"I use Contadina's Tomato Pesto for an extra burst of flavor. It's a low calorie dish."
Armida Gordon   **Fountain Valley High School, Fountain Valley, CA**

BAKED PARMESAN MACARONI
Serves 6

6 to 8 cups water
3 cups milk, preheated
3 tablespoons butter
3 tablespoons flour
$\frac{1}{2}$ teaspoon salt
dash Tabasco sauce
2 cups elbow macaroni
1 teaspoon salt
1 cup Parmesan cheese, grated
$\frac{1}{4}$ cup Romano cheese, grated
8 ounces mozzarella cheese, grated

Preheat oven to 350 degrees. Put water on to boil for macaroni. Place milk in microwave or stovetop to heat, 3 to 4 minutes. Heat butter in a saucepan until melted; stir in flour until smooth to dispel the raw taste of flour. Cook, stirring over low heat until roux is cooked, about 3 minutes. Gradually stir in the hot milk until smooth. Cook, stirring constantly until mixture boils and is thickened. Cook, stirring frequently over low heat, 10 minutes. Stir in salt and Tabasco sauce. Meanwhile, cook macaroni in boiling, salted water until al dente, about 8 minutes; drain. Combine the white sauce, cooked macaroni, Parmesan and Romano cheese until blended. Pour into buttered 9" x 13" baking dish. Sprinkle with mozzarella and bake at 350 degrees for 45 minutes.

Debbie Powers   **Griffiths Middle School, Downey, CA**

RIGATONI WITH ZUCCHINI & EGGPLANT
Serves 4

1 pound rigatoni pasta
1 (28 ounce) can Italian tomatoes
$\frac{1}{4}$ cup vegetable oil
1 eggplant, chopped
$\frac{1}{4}$ cup olive oil
1 clove garlic, diced
2 zucchini, halved, sliced $\frac{1}{3}$" thick
1 onion, thinly sliced
$\frac{1}{4}$ cup basil leaves, torn
1 teaspoon dried oregano
salt and pepper, to taste
$\frac{1}{2}$ pound mozzarella cheese, shredded
$\frac{1}{2}$ cup Parmesan cheese, freshly grated

Preheat oven to 350 degrees. Cook rigatoni in large pot of boiling water until al dente. Drain pasta and save $\frac{1}{4}$ cup cooking water for later. Puree tomatoes with their liquid; press through sieve to remove seeds. Heat vegetable oil in large nonstick skillet. Cook eggplant, half at a time, over medium-high heat, stirring occasionally, until golden, about 6 minutes. Using a slotted spoon, transfer eggplant to a plate lined with paper towels; discard oil left in pan. Heat olive oil in skillet; add garlic, zucchini and onion and cook over medium-high heat, stirring often until softened, about 6 minutes. Add tomato puree, basil and oregano and simmer over medium heat until sauce is reduced by one-third, about 15 minutes. Stir in eggplant and season with salt and pepper. Fold eggplant and zucchini sauce into rigatoni along with mozzarella cheese and reserved $\frac{1}{4}$ cup pasta cooking water. Transfer to a 9" x 13" baking dish. Sprinkle with Parmesan cheese and bake 15 minutes, or until heated through. Serve hot.

"I would like to credit Food & Wine *magazine for this excellent recipe."*
Carol O'Keefe   **Canyon High School, Anaheim, CA**

BAKED ZITI
Serves 4 - 6

    1 pound ziti
    12 ounces ricotta cheese
    2 eggs, beaten
    $\frac{3}{4}$ cup Parmesan cheese, grated, divided
    $\frac{1}{2}$ teaspoon salt
    $\frac{1}{4}$ teaspoon pepper
    2 tablespoons parsley
    3 cups marinara sauce, divided
    8 ounces mozzarella cheese, grated

Preheat oven to 350 degrees. Cook ziti in boiling, salted water until tender but still firm, 10 to 12 minutes. Drain and rinse under cold running water; drain well. In a medium bowl, combine ricotta cheese, eggs, $\frac{1}{2}$ cup Parmesan cheese, salt, pepper and parsley. Mix to blend well. Toss cooked ziti with 2 cups marinara sauce. Place half the pasta in an 11" x 17" baking dish. Top with ricotta mixture and half of the mozzarella cheese. Top with remaining ziti, marinara, mozzarella and Parmesan cheese. Bake until casserole is heated through and cheese is bubbly and lightly browned on top, 30 to 35 minutes.

"The closest I can get to an Italian restaurant in Brooklyn, New York!"
Patricia Zeitman   **Carlsbad High School, Carlsbad, CA**

BARBARA'S BOW TIE PASTA
Serves 3 - 4

    12 ounces bow tie pasta, cooked
    2 (6 ounce) packages fresh, baby spinach
    3 to 4 tablespoons olive oil
    4 Roma tomatoes, chopped
    3 to 4 tablespoons Parmesan cheese, freshly grated
    dash nutmeg

Prepare pasta according to package directions. Combine hot, cooked pasta with spinach until leaves are wilted. Add remaining ingredients and toss well.

"My friend, Barbara Jerele, of Food Professionals, made this dish for me."
Shelly Wellins   **Bolsa Grande High School, Garden Grove, CA**

EASY ARTICHOKE FRITTATA
Serves 6 - 8

>   3 cups artichoke hearts, chopped
>   ½ (medium) onion, chopped
>   1 clove garlic, minced
>   1 cup Bisquick
>   ½ cup vegetable oil
>   ½ teaspoon Italian seasoning
>   ½ teaspoon basil
>   ½ cup Parmesan cheese, grated
>   ¼ teaspoon seasoning salt
>   salt and pepper, to taste
>   4 eggs, beaten

Mix all ingredients in a large bowl, adding eggs last. (Mixture will be soupy.) Pour into a 9" x 13" oiled pan. Bake at 350 degrees for 25 to 30 minutes.

"Easy and delicious appetizer! Can be served as a main dish, accompanied by a salad!"

Charlene Nugent   **Petaluma Junior High School, Petaluma, CA**

EASY EGGPLANT PARMESAN
Serves 4

>   1 (large) or 2 (medium) eggplant
>   3 tablespoons oil
>   1 (16 ounce) jar spaghetti sauce
>   1 pound mozzarella cheese, shredded
>   *Garnish:* Parmesan cheese, grated

Grease a 9" x 13" pan. Peel eggplant and slice ¼" thick. Fry in oil until golden brown. Layer eggplant in pan, cover with sauce and sprinkle with mozzarella. Repeat until all ingredients are used, ending with mozzarella. Sprinkle with Parmesan. Bake at 375 degrees 15 to 25 minutes, until cheese melts.

"My high school students who think they hate eggplant love this!"

Sheri Rader   **Chaparral High School, Las Vegas, NV**

EASY PASTA PRIMAVERA
Serves 4 - 6

>   1 pound angel hair pasta
>   2 cups broccoli, fresh or frozen
>   8 ounces frozen mixed vegetables
>   1 jar pasta sauce, white, cheese variety

Boil spaghetti in large pan of water until al dente. While spaghetti cooks, microwave fresh or frozen vegetables until tender; drain. Add pasta sauce to vegetables. Drain spaghetti and toss with vegetables and sauce. Serve.

"Convenience foods help make a special dish in a hurry!"

Sue Fullmer   **Mojave High School, N. Las Vegas, NV**

EGGPLANT PASTA

Serves 6

2 small eggplants, chopped into ½" cubes (about 5 to 6 cups)
1 large onion, chopped
¼ cup olive oil, divided
4 stalks celery, sliced
2 (large) green bell peppers, chopped
2 to 4 cloves garlic, minced
1 (28 ounce) can diced tomatoes, with juice
3 to 4 tablespoons red wine vinegar
½ teaspoon salt
pepper, to taste
8 ounces rotelle pasta, cooked
¼ cup Parmesan cheese, grated

Soak eggplant in salted water 15 minutes; drain. Meanwhile, saute onion in 2 tablespoons olive oil. Add celery and saute until bright green. Add peppers and garlic; saute 2 to 3 minutes. Add tomatoes with their liquid, vinegar and salt. Remove from pan and set aside. Add remaining oil to pan and saute eggplant until tender. Return tomato mixture to pan and heat through. Serve over cooked rotelle and garnish with cheese.

"Lowfat, quick and healthy! You could eat it every day!"
Elizabeth Williams   **Chino High School, Chino , CA**

FETTUCCINI ALFREDO

Serves 4 - 6

8 ounces wide noodles or fettuccini pasta
2 tablespoons olive oil
2 tablespoons margarine
1 to 2 cloves garlic, minced (to taste)
½ cup cream
¼ cup Parmesan cheese, grated
½ teaspoon salt
dash white pepper
Garnish: Parmesan cheese, freshly grated

Bring 8 cups water to boil; add noodles and cook, uncovered until tender, about 5 to 7 minutes. Drain and return to pan; cover to keep warm. When noodles are nearly done, start sauce in small saucepan. Heat oil, margarine and garlic over low heat until sizzling. Stir in cream, cheese, salt and pepper; heat just until mixture boils. Remove from heat immediately. Pour sauce over cooked noodles, stirring until well coated. Top with freshly grated Parmesan cheese.

Optional: Broiled chicken, mushrooms or broccoli stirred into the sauce and served over the noodles tastes great and adds nutritional value. Also, freshly grated Parmesan cheese on top of it all is a must!

"A quick, easy family and classroom favorite!"
Charlotte Heitzmann   **Mariposa County High School, Mariposa, CA**

FETTUCCINI SPINACH TOSS

Serves 4

>   6 ounces noodles
>   1 ½ quarts boiling salted water
>   2 tablespoons butter
>   1 clove garlic, minced
>   1 teaspoon basil
>   ⅛ teaspoon salt
>   2 tablespoons flour
>   1 cup milk
>   1 (10 ounce) frozen chopped spinach, thawed
>   ½ cup Parmesan cheese, grated
>   1 pint cottage cheese

Cook noodles in water for 7 minutes; drain and set aside. Meanwhile, melt butter in skillet. Add garlic, basil, salt and flour, stirring until smooth. Stir milk into garlic mixture. Cook over medium-high heat, stirring constantly until mixture thickens and boils. Place spinach in a fine colander; press out water until dry. Add spinach and Parmesan cheese to sauce, stirring until cheese melts. Gently toss with noodles and cottage cheese. Heat thoroughly. Garnish with more Parmesan cheese, if desired.

DeLisa Davis   **Sutter High School, Sutter, CA**

FRESH TOMATOES WITH FETTUCCINI

Serves 8

>   1 pound fettuccini
>   4 (medium) ripe tomatoes, diced
>   1 (medium) red onion, chopped
>   2 cloves garlic, pressed
>   ¾ cup fresh basil, shredded
>   1 cup fresh parsley, chopped
>   1 cup feta cheese, coarsely crumbled
>   6 tablespoons olive oil
>   4 teaspoons balsamic vinegar
>   ¼ cup black olives, sliced
>   salt and pepper, to taste

Cook fettuccini according to package directions; drain. Combine remaining ingredients and toss with cooked fettuccini. Serve warm, cold or at room temperature.

"A great summer dinner. My family loves this served warm."

Judy Herman   **Dublin High School, Dublin, CA**

Leeks look like large green onions and have a mild onion flavor. To prepare, wash under cold running water. Trim off root ends and 2/3 of the green tops. Rinse again and cut into thin slices.

Jeri Drake Lane   **Canyon Springs HS, Moreno Valley, CA**

FRUIT & NUT PASTA BAKE
Serves 3 - 4

    2 cups spaghetti sauce, divided
    2 eggs, beaten
    ½ cup plain yogurt
    ½ cup raisins
    2 tablespoons parsley, chopped
    ½ teaspoon basil leaves, crushed
    ¼ teaspoon ground nutmeg
    ½ cup walnuts, chopped
    1 ½ cups jack cheese, grated
    4 ounces manicotti, uncooked
    ½ cup water
    Garnish: Parmesan cheese, grated

Pour 1 cup spaghetti sauce in shallow 2 quart baking pan. Combine eggs, yogurt, raisins, parsley, basil, nutmeg, walnuts and jack cheese. Stuff into uncooked noodles. Arrange in pan and cover with remaining spaghetti sauce and water. Cover tightly and bake 1 hour at 350 degrees. Sprinkle with grated Parmesan cheese.

Venetta Ramm   **La Habra High School, La Habra, CA**

ITALIAN GREEN BEANS WITH CANNELLINI
Serves 4

    1 pound small white or yellow boiling onions
    2 tablespoons olive oil
    1 yellow onion, coarsely chopped
    2 cloves garlic, finely chopped
    1 pound Italian (Romano) green beans,
        ends trimmed, cut on diagonal into 2" lengths
    4 long Italian green sweet peppers, seeded,
        cut lengthwise, into strips ½" wide
    1 (20 ounce) can cannellini, Great Northern or
        white kidney beans, drained
    6 large plum tomatoes, quartered
    ½ cup small black olives, pitted
    1 tablespoon fresh oregano leaves or 1 teaspoon dried
    1 tablespoon fresh basil or 1 teaspoon dried
    salt and freshly ground pepper, to taste

Using a sharp knife, trim ends of boiling onions. Cut a shallow X in each trimmed end (to keep onions whole during cooking). In a pot, combine the onions with plenty of water to cover; bring to a boil. Boil 2 minutes, then drain and when cool enough to handle, slip off skins. Set onions aside. In 4 quart heavy bottomed pot over medium heat, warm the olive oil. Add chopped onion and garlic and saute, stirring until onion is translucent, about 5 minutes. Add green beans, sweet peppers and reserved boiling onions. Continue to saute until peppers just start to soften, about 5 minutes longer. Add the canned beans, tomatoes, olives, oregano and basil. Cover and cook over medium-low heat until green beans are tender, about 15 minutes. Season with salt and pepper. Spoon into warmed shallow bowls and serve.

Toni Purtill   **Basic High School, Henderson, NV**

LASAGNA
Serves 6

6 lasagna noodles
1 tablespoon oil
1 1/2 cups pasta sauce
2 eggs
1 cup ricotta cheese
3 tablespoons green onion, minced
1 tablespoon parsley, minced
3/4 teaspoon salt
1/2 pound mozzarella cheese, grated
1/4 cup Parmesan cheese, shredded

Cook noodles in lightly salted water adding 1 tablespoon oil; cook 8 minutes. Rinse and drain. Cover the bottom of an 11" x 7" x 2" baking dish with a thin layer of pasta sauce. Beat eggs in a bowl. Blend in ricotta, green onion, parsley and salt. In baking dish layer in the following order: noodles, ricotta mixture, mozzarella, Parmesan, then sauce. Repeat layers. Top with Parmesan cheese. Cover and refrigerate 1 to 2 days or bake at once, at 350 degrees 30 to 35 minutes. Let stand 10 to 15 minutes before cutting.

Cheryl Clubb   **Saddleback High School, Santa Ana, CA**

LASAGNA ROLL-UPS
Makes 6 roll-ups

6 to 8 lasagna noodles, cooked
2 cups prepared pasta sauce
1 cup cottage cheese
1/4 cup Parmesan cheese, freshly grated
1 cup mozzarella cheese, grated, divided
1 egg, beaten
1 tablespoon parsley

Cook lasagna noodles according to package directions; drain and set aside. Preheat oven to 35 degrees. Pour 1 cup pasta sauce in bottom of 13" x 9" baking dish and spread to cover; set aside. Mix together cottage cheese, Parmesan cheese and 1/2 cup mozzarella (reserving 1/2 cup mozzarella cheese for topping). Add egg and parsley to make filling. Place a large spoonful of filling on a cooked lasagna noodle and roll up like a pinwheel. Place, seam side down in prepared pan. Continue until all ingredients are used. Cover with remaining 1 cup pasta sauce and top with reserved 1/2 cup mozzarella. Bake 20 to 25 minutes.

Elizabeth Ward   **Taft Union High School, Taft, CA**
Ruth Rimmer   **Dinuba High School, Dinuba, CA**

Italians are known for their gelatos. Fresh Orange Gelato can also be made with tangerines.

Judy Henry   **Newhart MS, Mission Viejo, CA**

Lasagna Roll-Ups with Spinach

Makes 6 roll ups

6 lasagna noodles
1 (28 ounce) can marinara sauce
2 cups ricotta cheese
1 cup mozzarella cheese, grated
1/4 cup Parmesan cheese, grated
1 egg, lightly beaten
1/2 package frozen spinach, chopped
nonstick cooking spray

Preheat oven to 350 degrees. Prepare lasagna noodles according to package directions; drain and set aside. While noodles are cooking, heat marinara sauce in a small saucepan. In a bowl, combine ricotta, mozzarella, Parmesan and egg; mix well. Squeeze liquid from spinach, add to cheese mixture and stir well. Divide mixture between noodles and spread evenly over entire length. Roll up and place seam side down in a baking dish that has been coated with nonstick cooking spray. Pour marinara sauce over top and bake 20 minutes.

"The students always like to make these at home because they look very showy when served."

Elaine Thomas **Kerman High School, Kerman, CA**

Leftover Pasta Frittata

Serves 4

5 tablespoons butter or margarine, divided
5 to 6 eggs
1 1/2 cups leftover cooked pasta
1/2 cup Parmesan cheese, grated
salt, pepper, seasonings, to taste

Heat 3 tablespoons butter or margarine in a pan until foamy. Combine eggs, pasta, Parmesan and seasonings in a bowl and mix well. Pour mixture into pan of heated butter or margarine. Allow to cook, without stirring, 5 minutes. After 5 minutes has passed, use a plate to slide the partially cooked frittata out of pan. Put the remaining butter or margarine in pan and melt until foamy. Place uncooked side of frittata onto pan and cook 5 to 8 minutes. Shake pan back and forth to loosen. Slide onto plate and enjoy.

"After she left school mid-semester a student showed up on my doorstep saying how much she really had enjoyed the class and had continued to do cooking on her own."

Nancy Cumming **Mt. Miguel High School, Spring Valley, CA**

Pesto was created in Genoa, a region known for the use of fresh herbs, vegetables and seafood

Alicia Pucci **Kenilworth JHS, Petaluma, CA**

LEMONY PASTA SALAD
Serves 8

1 (large) lemon
¼ cup olive oil
1 cup almonds, slivered
3 cups leeks, sliced
½ teaspoon salt
⅛ teaspoon pepper
1 red bell pepper, roasted, cut into strips
1 yellow bell pepper, roasted, cut into strips
8 ounces (3 ½ cups) bow tie pasta, uncooked

Remove peel from lemon; set aside. Cut off white pith and discard. Cut lemon into ¼" slices and set aside. Heat oil in large skillet. Add almonds and cook, stirring over high heat, 30 seconds until light brown. Remove almonds from pan. Add leeks, lemon slices and peel, salt and pepper. Cook and stir over high heat 1 minute or until vegetables are crisp tender; remove from heat. Remove lemon slices and discard. Stir in peppers and almonds, cover and refrigerate until chilled. Cook pasta to desired doneness; drain and rinse with cold water. Combine pasta with vegetables and toss gently.

Jeri Drake Lane   **Canyon Springs High School, Moreno Valley, CA**

LINGUINE & MUSHROOMS
Serves 3

⅓ cup olive oil
½ cube butter
¾ package linguine
3 cloves garlic, chopped
2 cups mushrooms, sliced
salt and pepper, to taste
dash red pepper flakes (optional)
½ cup Parmesan or Romano cheese, grated
½ cup parsley, chopped

Heat olive oil and melt butter in saucepan over low heat. Meanwhile, cook linguine according to package directions. Add garlic and mushrooms to oil and butter, stirring so garlic doesn't burn. Add salt and pepper, to taste. Add red pepper flakes, if desired. After a few minutes, lower heat. Drain pasta well, and add to sauce; toss. Sprinkle with grated Parmesan cheese and top with parsley.

Bill Bertrand   **Alta Loma High School, Alta Loma, CA**

LOWFAT MANICOTTI
Serves 6 - 8

3 eggs (may use egg substitute)
2 pounds nonfat ricotta cheese
¾ cup nonfat Parmesan cheese
½ pound nonfat mozzarella cheese, shredded
24 ounces spaghetti sauce
14 crepes

Mix eggs, ricotta, Parmesan and mozzarella in a bowl. Pour a small amount of spaghetti sauce in bottom of baking dish, spreading to cover bottom. Fill crepes with cheese filling and place in baking dish. Pour remaining sauce over crepes. Bake 45 minutes at 350 degrees.

Debra Marvulli   **Merced High School, Merced, CA**

MANICOTTI WITH CHEESE FILLING
Serves 6 - 8

    1 (8 ounce) package manicotti
    2 cups mozzarella cheese, shredded
    2 cups (15 ounces) ricotta cheese
    1/4 cup Parmesan cheese, grated
    2 tablespoons parsley, chopped
    1/2 teaspoon salt
    1/4 teaspoon pepper
    1 (32 ounce) jar spaghetti sauce

Cook manicotti according to package directions; drain. Cool in single layer on waxed paper or aluminum foil to prevent manicotti from sticking together. Combine cheeses, parsley, salt and pepper for filling. Spoon filling into manicotti. Spread a thin layer of sauce on bottom of a 9" x 13" baking pan. Arrange manicotti in single layer over sauce. Cover with remaining sauce. Cover with aluminum foil. Bake at 350 degrees for about 40 minutes. Remove foil; baking 15 minutes longer.

Liz Williams   **Ontario High School, Ontario, CA**

MAXINE'S MANICOTTI
Serves 4 - 6

    1 (8 ounce) package jumbo shells
    1 tablespoon olive oil
    2 eggs, slightly beaten
    1/2 pound mozzarella cheese, diced
    1/2 cup cottage cheese
    1/2 cup + 2 tablespoon Parmesan cheese, grated, divided
    1 jar spaghetti sauce

Cook shells according to package directions, adding 1 tablespoon olive oil to cooking water. While shells cook, combine eggs, mozzarella cheese, cottage cheese, 2 tablespoons Parmesan cheese and salt in a bowl; mix thoroughly. Place a light layer of your favorite spaghetti sauce in shallow rectangular baking dish. Stuff each shell with egg/cheese mixture and place in pan. Cover with remaining sauce. Sprinkle liberally with 1/2 cup Parmesan cheese and bake at 375 degrees for 20 minutes.

"Handed-down version from my Aunt Maxine. We've enjoyed it for years."

Susan Sullins   **Central Middle School, Oroville, CA**

Mushroom Frittata

Serves 4

Photo opposite page 64

1 teaspoon butter or margarine
1 (medium) zucchini, grated
1 (medium) tomato, chopped
1 (4 ounce) can mushrooms, sliced, drained
6 eggs, beaten
1/4 cup milk
3/4 teaspoon Lawry's Seasoned Salt
1/2 teaspoon Lawry's Seasoned Pepper
2 cups Swiss cheese, shredded
2 teaspoons Dijon mustard

In large nonstick skillet, melt butter or margarine. Add zucchini, tomato and mushrooms; cook 1 minute. In large bowl, combine remaining ingredients. Add egg mixture to skillet; mix well. Cover and cook 10 minutes over low heat. To brown top, place skillet under broiler 2 to 3 minutes. Slice frittata onto serving dish.

"The perfect late night supper or lazy morning meal."

Lawry's Foods, Inc.   **Monrovia, CA**

Oh! So Good!

Serves 8 - 10

3 medium zucchini
1 pound Monterey jack cheese, divided
nonstick cooking spray
2 cups medium-size pasta, cooked
1 (7 ounce) can green chiles
1 (large) tomato, sliced
1 (medium) red bell pepper, chopped
1 (medium) yellow bell pepper, chopped
1 to 2 cups mushrooms, sliced
2 cups sour cream
1 teaspoon garlic salt
1 teaspoon parsley
1 teaspoon oregano
salt and pepper, to taste
2 teaspoons green onion, chopped

Slice and slightly steam zucchini; set aside. Divide cheese in half; cut half into strips, and grate the other half; set aside. Spray a 9" x 13" x 2" casserole dish with nonstick cooking spray. Layer in the following order: cooked pasta, chiles, cheese strips, zucchini, tomatoes, red bell pepper, yellow bell pepper and mushrooms. Mix together sour cream with spices and green onion; pour over vegetables. Sprinkle shredded cheese over top. Bake at 350 degrees for 30 minutes.

"The key is the cheese and sour cream mixture. Try adding chicken too!"

Brenda Burke   **Mt. Whitney High School, Visalia, CA**

PASTA & BEANS
Serves 4 - 5

- 1 (16 ounce) can pinto beans
- 1 (16 ounce) can beef bouillon
- 3 cloves garlic, whole
- 3 stalks celery, cut into 4″ strips
- ¼ cup olive oil
- ¼ cup onion, chopped
- 2 to 3 cups salad macaroni noodles
- 2 to 3 tablespoons tomato sauce
- salt and pepper, to taste

Combine pinto beans with beef bouillon, garlic and celery in saucepan. Cook 30 minutes to 1 hour. Remove garlic and celery. In small fry pan, fry olive oil and onion together until translucent. Add to beans. Stir in tomato sauce. Cook noodles according to package directions. Drain, then mix together with beans. Salt and pepper to taste.

"We had this once a week while I was growing up in our Italian family."
Ruth Schletewitz   **Rafer Johnson Junior High School, Kingsburg, CA**

PASTA FAGIOLI
Serves 8 - 10

- 1 medium onion, chopped
- 3 cloves garlic, peeled, sliced
- 1 tablespoon vegetable oil
- 1 teaspoon olive oil
- 10 leaves fresh basil leaves, chopped
- 1 bay leaf
- 1 ½ teaspoons salt
- 2 tablespoons oregano
- 4 (15 ounce) cans Northern white beans, drained
- 2 cups water
- 5 (8 ounce) cans tomato sauce
- 1 ½ pounds elbow macaroni, cooked, drained
- *Garnish:* Parmesan cheese, freshly grated

Fry onion and garlic in a large pot with vegetable oil and olive oil, 7 to 10 minutes. Add basil, bay leaf, salt, and oregano and coat with oil. Stir in drained beans, water and tomato sauce. Simmer 1 ½ to 2 hours, adding water as needed. (Should be a thick soup - you can mash the beans if desired, to thicken.) After 2 hours, stir in pasta, which has been cooked according to package directions. Serve immediately, garnished with freshly grated Parmesan cheese.

"Freeze half of the sauce, without the macaroni, and save it for another meal.
Thanks to Katie Placido for sharing her family recipe!"
Rhonda Nelson   **Rancho Santa Margarita Intermediate School,**
Rancho Santa Margarita, CA

Pasta Pizza Casserole

Serves 8 - 10

1 pound elbow macaroni
nonstick cooking spray
1 tablespoon Italian seasoning
2 cloves garlic, minced
½ teaspoon crushed red pepper
1 (8 ounce) can tomato sauce
¼ cup Parmesan cheese, shredded
1 (15 ounce) can crushed tomatoes
2 cups any combination of fresh chopped vegetables
    (such as carrots, celery, zucchini)
½ cup garbanzo beans, rinsed and drained
¼ cup sliced olives (optional)
1 cup mozzarella cheese, grated

Preheat oven to 400 degrees. In a large pot of boiling water, cook pasta until just underdone; drain. Place pasta in a 9" x 13" baking pan that has been coated with nonstick cooking spray. Toss pasta with Italian seasoning, garlic, crushed red pepper, tomato sauce and Parmesan cheese. Pour crushed tomatoes over top, then layer remaining ingredients, ending with shredded mozzarella. Bake 25 minutes or until bubbly. Serve hot.

Janet Dukes　　　　　**Newport Harbor High School, Newport Beach, CA**

Pasta Primavera

Serves 4

nonstick cooking spray
2 cups mushrooms, sliced
2 (large) cloves garlic, minced
2 carrots, peeled, sliced ¼" thick
⅔ cup dry white wine or vegetable broth
1 cup broccoli florets
½ cup frozen peas
1 (large) tomato, diced
⅓ cup walnuts, toasted, coarsely chopped
2 tablespoons dried basil leaves
1 (8 ounce) package penne pasta, cooked, drained, kept warm
salt and pepper, to taste
⅓ cup Parmesan cheese, shredded

Coat a large nonstick skillet with cooking spray; set over medium heat. Add mushrooms and garlic; saute 1 minute. Cover skillet; simmer 5 minutes. Add carrots and wine or vegetable broth; bring to a boil. Cover and simmer 5 minutes. Stir in broccoli and peas; cover and simmer 2 minutes. Stir in tomato, walnuts and basil; warm through. In a bowl, toss pasta with sauce, season with salt and pepper and toss with cheese.

"My family has been growing Diamond walnuts for 52 years.
Thanks to them for this delicious, colorful, low calorie main dish recipe!"
Carole Delap　　　　　**Golden West High School, Visalia, CA**

Pasta with Fresh Tomatoes & Pesto
Serves 6

¼ cup pesto
3 cups fresh tomatoes, diced OR 3 cups canned
tomatoes, drained, diced
1 pound short pasta
Garnish: Parmesan or Romano cheese, grated

Gently mix pesto with tomatoes in large pasta serving bowl. Let stand while you cook pasta. Cook pasta al dente; drain. Toss gently with pesto and tomatoes. Serve hot or warm with grated cheese.

"Fresh tomatoes straight from the garden are the best, but canned, diced tomatoes in juice will do. Drain tomatoes before measuring."

Ashley Nelson   **Holmes Junior High School, Davis, CA**

Pastitsio
Serves 6

½ pound pasta shells
1 tablespoon olive oil
Cheese Sauce:
3 tablespoons olive oil
2 tablespoons flour
1 ½ cups 1% milk
¼ teaspoon salt
¼ teaspoon pepper
pinch nutmeg
2 eggs, beaten
1 cup Parmesan cheese, grated
2 cups spaghetti sauce
Garnish: ¼ cup Parmesan cheese, grated

Cook pasta according to package directions; drain and toss with 1 tablespoon olive oil; set aside. Make cheese sauce: Warm 3 tablespoons olive oil in a medium saucepan. Whisk continuously while adding flour to dissolve and slowly add milk and seasonings; bring to a simmer. Remove from heat and stir in eggs and 1 cup Parmesan cheese. Preheat oven to 350 degrees. Place half the pasta in a greased 11" x 17" casserole dish. Layer with half the sauce; repeat. Sprinkle with ¼ cup Parmesan cheese and bake 35 to 40 minutes.

"The class thought this was the best spaghetti casserole they had ever tasted!"

Mabel Chase   **Ventura High School, Ventura, CA**

Penne with Fontina Cheese
Serves 4

8 ounces penne pasta
salt and pepper, to taste
4 ounces fontina cheese, thinly sliced
¼ cup butter
2 teaspoons fresh oregano, chopped

Preheat oven to 400 degrees. Butter an 8" x 11" glass baking dish. Cook pasta in large pot of boiling water until tender but still firm to bite; drain. Arrange ⅓ of pasta in bottom of baking dish. Sprinkle with salt and pepper. Arrange ½ of cheese slices over pasta; repeat layers. Top with remaining pasta. Sprinkle with salt and pepper. Dot with butter. Bake pasta, uncovered, about 10 minutes, until cheese melts. Toss; bake 2 minutes more. Season to taste. Sprinkle chopped oregano on top and serve immediately.

"This is more sophisticated than mom's mac and cheese, but just as good.
Use a cheese slicer to get thin, even slices of this delicious cheese."
Delaine Smith   **West Valley High School, Cottonwood, CA**

PISTACHIO PASTA
Serves 4 - 6
- 1 (8 ounce) box penne pasta, cooked, drained
- 2 tablespoons butter
- 1 (large) yellow onion, thinly sliced
- ½ cup green bell pepper, diced
- ½ cup red bell pepper, diced
- 1 small can olives, sliced
- 2 tablespoons garlic, minced
- ¼ pound prosciutto, diced
- 1 cup pistachios, coarsely chopped
- 1 ½ teaspoons dried rosemary, crumbled
- ½ cup extra virgin olive oil
- 4 ounces blue cheese, crumbled

Prepare pasta according to package directions. Melt butter. Saute onion until tender. Add peppers, garlic, prosciutto, pistachios, olives, rosemary and olive oil to skillet. Continue cooking, stirring until hot. Add crumbled blue cheese. Toss with pasta and serve.

"Northern Italian dish. Great with hot crusty sourdough bread and salad!"
Kris Hawkins   **Clovis West High School, Fresno, CA**

QUICK & EASY VEGETARIAN LASAGNA
Serves 12
- 1 (1 pound, 10 ounce) jar vegetables spaghetti sauce
- 1 (16 ounce) package lasagna noodles, cooked
- 1 (10 ounce) package frozen chopped spinach,
    thawed and squeezed dry
- 8 eggs, hard boiled, sliced
- 2 (5 ounce) packages mozzarella cheese, sliced
- ½ cup Parmesan cheese, grated

Pour enough sauce to cover the bottom of an 11" x 13" baking dish. Line with one row cooked noodles. Top with a layer of sauce, spinach, eggs, and mozzarella cheese. Repeat noodles through cheese until pan has three layers. Finish with a layer of noodles, sauce and Parmesan cheese. Bake at 350 degrees 30 to 35 minutes.

"Sometimes I make this recipe one day in advance."
Sandi Coulter   **San Juan High School, Citrus Heights, CA**

Ravioli with Roasted Red Pepper Cream
Serves 4

1 (25 ounce) package frozen cheese ravioli
1 (7 ounce) jar roasted red peppers, drained
½ cup white wine
1 cup heavy or whipping cream
¾ cup Parmesan cheese, freshly grated

Cook ravioli according to package directions. Meanwhile, heat peppers and wine in a saucepan to a boil. Continue to cook until only about 2 tablespoons liquid remains, 4 to 5 minutes. Add the cream, return to a boil, stirring constantly to thicken slightly. Remove from heat. Add Parmesan and stir until melted. Pour sauce over cooked ravioli.

Maria Montemagni   **Mt. Whitney High School, Visalia, CA**

Rigatoni with Eggplant & Tomatoes
Serves 4 - 6

1 medium eggplant, cut into 1" cubes
1 tablespoon salt
⅓ cup olive oil
1 cup (oil packed) sun dried tomatoes, loosely packed (reserve oil)
2 tablespoons reserved oil
3 tablespoons fresh parsley, chopped
½ pound dry rigatoni noodles
2 ounces fresh goat cheese, crumbled
Garnish: Parmesan cheese, freshly grated

Preheat oven to 450 degrees. Place eggplant cubes in a colander; sprinkle lightly with salt. Allow eggplant to stand about 30 minutes; drain. Pour olive oil into baking dish. Add eggplant and toss well to coat. Place pan in oven and roast, stirring occasionally, until eggplant is well browned, about 20 minutes. Meanwhile, chop sun dried tomatoes. Add reserved oil and parsley; set aside. Boil noodles as directed on package. Drain and transfer to serving dish. Add roasted eggplant and sun dried tomato mixture; toss well. Sprinkle goat cheese on top and serve with Parmesan.

Donna Leslie   **Menlo-Atherton HS, Menlo Park, CA**

Spaghetti al Pomodori
Serves 5

4 tablespoons (½ stick) butter
¼ cup onion, finely chopped
¼ cup carrots, finely diced
¼ cup celery, finely diced
2 cups (canned) whole peeled tomatoes, with juice, coarsely chopped
salt, to taste
1 pound cooked pasta

Melt butter in a saucepan over medium-low heat. Add onion, carrots, celery and saute until softened. Add tomatoes and salt; simmer 20 to 30 minutes. Serve with cooked spaghetti, angel hair pasta, linguine, or fettuccini.

"This is the favorite recipe of my family and an easy way to increase veggie servings!"
Nanci Burkhart   **Hueneme High School, Oxnard, CA**

SPAGHETTI SARDI

Serves 4

    2 tablespoons olive oil
    1 tablespoon red onion, chopped
    2 (small) cans tomato sauce
    1 tablespoon fresh Italian parsley
    1 chunk Romano cheese, grated
    1 leaf basil
    1 pound spaghetti
    2 teaspoons salt
    1 chunk Parmigiana cheese, grated

Saute onions in olive oil. When browned, add tomato sauce, parsley, half of the Romano cheese and basil. Let simmer 15 minutes. Meanwhile, boil spaghetti in large container with salt added to water. Boil until al dente; drain. Add more of each cheese to sauce and pour over spaghetti; toss. Add more cheese to top and serve.

"Eat, eat, eat. Caoi! (from ESL teacher from Italy)!"

Maria Angela Miller   **Mojave High School, N. Las Vegas, NV**

SPINACH ARTICHOKE PIE

Serves 6 - 8

    3 tablespoons vegetable oil, divided
    1/4 cup bread crumbs
    1/2 pound fresh mushrooms, sliced
    1 pound fresh spinach, cooked, chopped
    1 (6.5 ounce) jar marinated artichoke hearts, drained, quartered
    1 cup day old bread cubes
    1 1/4 cups cheddar cheese, shredded, divided
    1 (4 ounce) jar pimientos, diced, drained
    2 eggs, beaten
    1/4 to 1/2 teaspoon garlic powder

Brush the bottom and sides of a 9" pie plate with 2 tablespoons oil; sprinkle with bread crumbs and set aside. In a skillet, saute mushrooms in remaining oil; drain and remove from heat. Squeeze spinach dry, add to mushrooms. Stir in artichokes, bread cubes, 1 cup shredded cheese, pimientos, eggs and garlic powder; stir well. Spoon into prepared pie plate. Bake, uncovered, at 350 degrees for 30 minutes. Sprinkle with remaining cheese and bake 5 to 10 minutes longer, or until cheese is melted. Let stand 10 minutes before cutting.

"I got this recipe from my favorite cooking magazine, Taste Of Home. *My husband and I love this recipe. It makes a great light dinner, with lots of flavor!"*

Julie Eyre   **Alhambra High School, Alhambra, CA**

Arborio rice is a special rice used for Italian cooking. It is the best for risotto. Risotto is a creamy style Italian rice from Northern Italy.

Patti Bartholomew   **Casa Roble HS, Orangevale, CA**

STUFFED BUTTERNUT SQUASH
Serves 2 - 4

1 butternut squash
1 cup nonfat ricotta cheese
$\frac{1}{4}$ cup Parmesan cheese, grated
$\frac{1}{2}$ cup mozzarella cheese, grated
$\frac{1}{2}$ cup Italian style bread crumbs
2 tablespoons fresh parsley, minced
1 egg
$\frac{1}{2}$ cup nuts, chopped (pine nuts or walnuts)
1 teaspoon salt
$\frac{1}{2}$ teaspoon pepper

Cut squash in half and lay in a microwave-safe dish. Put $\frac{1}{4}$" water in bottom of dish and cover with plastic wrap. Microwave 10 to 20 minutes or until squash is tender. Scrape out inside of squash and mash in large bowl. Add all remaining ingredients, reserving $\frac{1}{4}$ cup of mozzarella cheese for topping. Scoop mixture back into squash shells and bake 20 minutes at 350 degrees. Sprinkle remaining cheese on top and serve.

Alicia Thomas   **Fallbrook High School, Fallbrook, CA**

STUFFED SHELLS FLORENTINE
Serves 4

2 tablespoons corn oil
$\frac{1}{2}$ cup onion, chopped
1 clove garlic, crushed
1 (28 ounce) can crushed tomatoes
1 (6 ounce) can tomato paste
1 tablespoon + 2 teaspoons parsley flakes
$\frac{1}{2}$ teaspoon oregano leaves
1 teaspoon basil leaves
$\frac{1}{8}$ teaspoon black pepper
1 (10 ounce) package frozen chopped spinach
1 (8 ounce) package (20 shells) large pasta shells
1 (15 ounce) container part skim ricotta cheese
1 cup mozzarella cheese, shredded
$\frac{1}{4}$ cup Parmesan cheese, grated

In a 3 quart saucepan, heat corn oil; saute onion and garlic over medium heat. Stir in tomatoes, tomato paste, 1 tablespoon parsley, oregano, $\frac{1}{2}$ teaspoon basil and pepper. Heat sauce to boiling. Reduce heat to medium-low setting and simmer, uncovered, stirring frequently, for about 30 minutes, or until sauce thickens. Cook spinach according to package directions; drain well, pressing out all water; set aside. Cook pasta shells according to package directions; drain and set aside. Combine cooked spinach, ricotta, mozzarella, 2 teaspoons parsley, and $\frac{1}{2}$ teaspoon basil in medium bowl. Stuff each shell with rounded tablespoon of cheese mixture. Pour 1 cup sauce in baking pan. Place stuffed shells on top of sauce, seam side up, in one layer. Spoon remaining sauce over shells, sprinkle with Parmesan. Bake at 350 degrees for 30 minutes.

"Add salad and bread and you have a delicious, meatless meal!"
Judy Hammann   **Mesa Junior High School, Mesa, AZ**

STUFFED SHELLS WITH TOFU
Serves 6

> 12 (jumbo) pasta shells
> 1 pound firm tofu
> 1 (10 ounce) box frozen spinach, thawed, squeezed dry
> ¼ cup fresh parsley, finely chopped
> ¼ cup Parmesan cheese, grated
> 2 tablespoons olive oil
> 1 teaspoon salt
> ⅛ teaspoon nutmeg
> 1 (32 ounce) jar pasta sauce

Cook pasta according to package directions; drain. Using a food processor, process tofu with spinach, parsley, Parmesan, oil, salt and nutmeg until well blended. Stuff shells with tofu mixture. Place in shallow baking pan and pour sauce over top. Cover with foil. Bake at 350 degrees for 30 minutes.

Joye Cantrell   **Rialto High School, Rialto, CA**

SUMMER FRITTATA
Serves 4

> ½ cup oil
> 9 eggs, lightly beaten
> salt and pepper, to taste
> 4 cloves garlic, peeled, minced
> 1(small) head broccoli, coarsely chopped
> ½ cup fresh porcini mushrooms, cleaned, thinly sliced

Heat all but 3 tablespoons olive oil in a heavy 10" skillet. Pour eggs into hot pan and cook over medium-low heat for 4 to 6 minutes, drawing the eggs away from the sides of the pan with a fork or small spatula so that the uncooked egg runs to the sides and cooks. Season with salt and pepper. Spread garlic, broccoli and mushrooms over eggs and cook 2 to 4 minutes longer. Heat remaining oil in a 12" skillet. Carefully loosen the frittata from the smaller skillet and flip into the larger one. Cook 3 to 4 minutes until eggs are cooked through.

Julie Daters   **Summerville Union High School, Tuolumne, CA**

SUMMER PASTA
Serves 4 - 6

> 1 pound fresh mozzarella cheese, cut into small cubes
> 8 (medium) tomatoes, diced
> 4 (large) cloves garlic, thinly sliced
> ¾ cup extra virgin olive oil
> 1 cup fresh basil, coarsely chopped
> salt, pepper and crushed red pepper, to taste
> 1 ½ pounds spaghetti or penne

In a bowl, toss mozzarella with tomatoes, garlic, olive oil, basil and salt. Season generously with pepper and crushed red pepper. Let stand about 30 minutes for flavors to blend. Prepare pasta according to package directions; drain. Return to pot, add sauce and toss well. Serve hot or at room temperature.

"Donated by the infamous Mr. Franklin, from San Marcos High School."
Marilyn Bankhead   **San Marcos High School, San Marcos, CA**

VEGETABLE LASAGNA
Serves 4 - 6

6 lasagna noodles
1 carrot, sliced
1 zucchini, sliced
½ onion, chopped
6 mushrooms, sliced
1 tablespoon oil
½ teaspoon basil
½ teaspoon oregano
16 ounces spaghetti sauce
1 (6 ounce) package frozen spinach, thawed, drained
¼ pound (½ cup) ricotta cheese
1 cup (4 ounces) mozzarella cheese, shredded

Fill a large pot halfway with water; cover and bring to boil. Wash and slice carrots and zucchini into ¼" slices. Add lasagna noodles and carrots to boiling water. Cook 6 minutes. Add zucchini to boiling water and cook 5 minutes longer. Drain pasta and vegetables into colander. In a large frying pan, heat oil. Cook onion, mushrooms, basil and oregano 5 to 8 minutes. Add spaghetti sauce to frying pan; set aside to cool. In a small bowl, combine spinach and ricotta cheese; set aside. To assemble lasagna: Spread one fourth of sauce mixture on bottom of square casserole dish. Arrange 3 noodles over sauce, (cut off excess with kitchen shears and use for top layer). Layer one third carrots and zucchini on top of noodles. Spread one third ricotta cheese and spinach mixture over vegetables. Sprinkle with one third mozzarella. Repeat layers. Spread sauce on top and sprinkle with Parmesan cheese. Bake, uncovered at 350 degrees for 45 minutes or microwave (covered with plastic wrap) at 70% power 12 minutes; rotate dish ½ turn and continue to cook 12 minutes more, or until bubbly. Let stand 15 minutes before serving.

"My students complain about making vegetable lasagna, and then they love it!"
Diane Lizardi   **Downey High School, Downey, CA**

VEGETARIAN PITA
Serves 4

1 ½ cups bean sprouts
⅓ cup Italian salad dressing
1 (medium) cucumber, peeled, chopped
1 (medium) tomato, chopped
10 ounces sharp cheddar cheese, grated
1 large carrot, shredded
4 (6") pita breads
lettuce leaves

Toss the beans sprouts with Italian dressing, cucumber and tomatoes; marinate 30 minutes at room temperature. Stir in cheese and carrots. Cut open pitas and fill with salad mixture. Add lettuce leaves and serve.

"Fresh Italian herbs may be used if desired - this is a good and easy lab!"
Lindy Cooper   **Simi Valley High School, Simi Valley, CA**

Lamb & Spinach Manicotti

New twist on an old favorite.

(page 82)

Toffee Tiramisu
Four layers of chocolate
and toffee bars. (page 144)

ZUCCHINI CASSEROLE
Serves 6 - 8

3 pounds zucchini
4 eggs, beaten
1/2 cup milk
1 (4 ounce) can green chiles, diced
1/4 cup parsley, chopped
1 pound Monterey Jack cheese, cubed
1 teaspoon salt
2 teaspoons baking powder
1 cup bread crumbs
2 tablespoons butter

Preheat oven to 350 degrees. Cube zucchini and steam until just barely tender. Combine eggs, milk, chiles, parsley, cheese, salt and baking powder. Toss in zucchini and mix well. Transfer to a buttered casserole that has been dusted with half of the bread crumbs, then sprinkle the top with remaining bread crumbs and dot with butter. Bake 45 minutes, or until cooked through and lightly browned.

Carol Helmle   **Tokay High School, Lodi, CA**

ZUCCHINI QUICHE ITALIAN PIE
Serves 4 - 6

1 (9") pie shell
2 tablespoons oil
2 cups zucchini, chopped
1/2 cup onion, chopped
1 clove garlic, minced
1 1/4 cups mozzarella cheese, shredded
3 eggs, beaten
1 cup cottage cheese
1/3 cup milk
1/2 teaspoon salt
1/2 teaspoon pepper
1 (15 ounce) can tomato sauce
1 tablespoon Italian seasoning
dash garlic powder

Preheat oven to 350 degrees. Bake pie shell 10 minutes; cool. Increase heat to 375 degrees. Heat oil in a medium pan over medium heat. Add zucchini, onion and garlic. Saute until tender, approximately 10 minutes. Spread into pie shell. In another bowl, mix 1 cup mozzarella, eggs, cottage cheese, milk, salt and pepper. Spoon over pie. Top with 1/4 cup mozzarella. Bake 40 minutes. Meanwhile, combine tomato sauce, Italian seasoning, and garlic powder in saucepan; simmer 15 minutes; keep warm. Let pie stand 5 minutes before serving; serve with heated tomato sauce.

"This is really yummy with a green salad and Italian bread!"

Cari Sheridan   **Grace Yokley School, Ontario, CA**

Desserts

AMARETTI (ALMOND COOKIES)
Makes 3 dozen

2 cups almonds, blanched
1 cup sugar
1 teaspoon almond extract
2 egg whites, beaten until stiff
confectioner's sugar

Grind almonds until fine. Spread on baking sheet, allowing to dry several hours. Combine almonds, sugar and almond extract; gently fold in beaten egg whites. Drop batter by teaspoonfuls onto greased and floured cookie sheets, allowing 2" between each cookie. Sprinkle with confectioner's sugar. Allow cookies to stand, uncovered, at room temperature to dry before baking, about 1 hour. Bake in preheated 325 degree oven 15 minutes or until golden brown. Cool on cookie sheets several minutes before removing to rack.

"These cookies can be frozen."

Kathie Baczynski   **Mt. Carmel High School, San Diego, CA**

AMARETTO BISCOTTI
Makes 4 - 5 dozen

1/2 cup butter
1 1/2 cups sugar
3 eggs
1 teaspoon Amaretto liqueur
1 tablespoon anise seed
1 teaspoon lemon rind, grated
1 cup walnuts, chopped
3 cups flour
3 teaspoons baking powder
1/2 teaspoon salt

Cream butter and sugar. Add beaten eggs, Amaretto, anise seed, lemon rind and walnuts. Add flour, which has been sifted with baking powder and salt. Knead into a roll, adding more flour so it won't stick. Cut into 5 rolls and shape into flattened loaves. Place on a greased cookie sheet. Bake at 350 degrees 25 to 30 minutes. Cool slightly; cut diagonally and put back in oven for about 10 minutes more.

"This recipe was given to me by a student of Italian descent. Her father made these cookies for a luncheon we had and was generous enough to share the family recipe!"

Debbie Grove   **Piner High School, Santa Rosa, CA**

APPLESAUCE PIZZA
Serves 6 - 8

2 cups Bisquick
1/2 cup water
3/4 cup applesauce
1/3 cup sugar
1/2 teaspoon cinnamon
1/8 teaspoon nutmeg
6 tablespoons flour
1/4 cup margarine

Preheat oven to 425 degrees. Measure biscuit mix into a bowl and stir in water lightly with a fork. Knead 5 times on a flour board. Tear off 10" wide piece of aluminum foil. Roll dough on foil in a circle. Turn up edge of foil and edge of dough 1/2" Spread applesauce on crust. Combine sugar, cinnamon, nutmeg and flour, cut margarine into mixture and crumble topping over applesauce. Bake 20 to 25 minutes. Cut and serve.

Jill Butler   **Canyon High School, Canyon Country, CA**

BISCOTTI
Makes 3 dozen

3 cups flour, sifted
1 teaspoon salt
1 tablespoon baking powder
1/2 cup butter or margarine
1 cup sugar
1 1/2 teaspoons anise oil
3 eggs
1 cup almonds, chopped and toasted

Preheat oven to 350 degrees. Sift dry ingredients together. In another bowl, cream butter, sugar and anise oil. Beat in eggs, one at at time. Add flour mixture to creamed mixture and blend. Stir in nuts. On a cookie sheet, form 2 rectangles, by rolling dough approximately 10" long, 4" wide, 1/2" thick. Bake until firm to touch, about 30 to 35 minutes. Turn off oven. Remove from oven and cool slightly. While warm, cut into 1/2" slices and separate. Return to oven (that is turned off) to dry out, about 10 to 20 minutes. Cool and store in a tin.

"Anise oil works the best. It gives the cookies a better flavor."

Cheri Schuette   **Valley View Middle School, Simi Valley, CA**
Amy Tavaliogne-Rudolph   **Etiwanda High School, Etiwanda, CA**

BISCUIT TORTONI
Serves 4 - 6

2 eggs, separated
1/2 cup powdered sugar, sifted
1 teaspoon rum extract
1/2 teaspoon vanilla
1 cup cream, whipped
1/2 cup + 3 tablespoons almond macaroons, crushed
1/4 cup maraschino cherries, chopped

Beat egg yolks with sugar until light and fluffy. Stir in rum and vanilla extracts. Beat egg whites until stiff. Gently fold into egg yolk mixture. Fold in whipped cream and half of the crushed macaroons, along with the cherries.Spoon mixture into individual dessert cups. Sprinkle each with remaining crushed macaroons. Freeze until firm. Serve with fresh summer fruit.

Janica Paustian   **College Park High School, Pleasant Hill, CA**

BLACK FOREST CAKE
Serves 12

1 box chocolate fudge cake mix
3 ounces cherry jello
¾ cup boiling water
½ cup cold water
3 tablespoons cherry chocolate liqueur
3 ounces chocolate pudding mix
2 envelops Dream Whip
1 ¼ cups cold milk
1 (21 ounce) can cherry pie filling

Prepare cake mix according to package directions; bake in a bundt or tube pan. Dissolve cherry jello in boiling water. Stir in cold water and cherry chocolate liqueur. Dot holes in cake with the end of a wooden spoon or similar tool. Pour jello over cake evenly filling holes and edges. Cover with plastic wrap and chill a minimum of 2 hours or overnight. Beat pudding mix and Dream Whip with milk on high until peaks form Ice cake with pudding mix. Fill center of cake with cherry pie filling.

"Not exactly Italian, but chocolate and cherries do go great with any Italian meal!"
Barbara Allen   **Ayala High School, Chino, CA**

CANNOLI
Serves 12

Pizzelles: (Cannoli)
2 eggs, well beaten
½ cup sugar
¼ cup butter, melted
¼ cup vegetable oil
¼ teaspoon baking soda
1 teaspoon cinnamon
1 tablespoon white vinegar
3 tablespoons cold water
1 ½ cups flour
Filling:
2 cups (approximately 1 pound) ricotta cheese
1 cup sugar, powdered or granulated
¼ cup semi-sweet chocolate
1 teaspoon vanilla
½ cup candied cherries
powdered sugar, for dusting

Pizzelles: Blend pizzelle ingredients together, adding one at a time. Pour batter in pizzelle iron and bake. Remove and roll hot cookie into a cylinder and allow to cool. *Filling:* Blend cheese and sugar until smooth. Add remaining ingredients. When pizzelles are cooled, fill with filling and sprinkle with powdered sugar.

Millie Deeton   **Ayala High School, Chino Hills, CA**

CAPPUCCINO

Serves 1

> 1/2 teaspoon sugar
> 1/2 teaspoon cocoa powder
> 2.5 ounces strong black coffee
> 2.5 ounces half & half
> 1 1/2 ounces brandy
> *Garnish:* Whipped cream

Combine sugar and cocoa. Mix with coffee and half & half in 8 ounce serving glass. Add brandy and top with whipped cream.

Kathie Baczynski   **Mt. Carmel High School, San Diego, CA**

CHOCOLATE ALMOND CHEESECAKE

Serves 12

> 1 1/2 cups chocolate wafers, crushed
> 1 cup almonds, toasted, chopped
> 1 1/3 cups + 1 tablespoon sugar, divided
> 3/4 stick butter, softened
> 1 1/2 pounds cream cheese
> 4 eggs
> 1/3 cup heavy cream
> 1/4 cup Amaretto
> 1 teaspoon vanilla
> 2 cups sour cream
> 1 teaspoon vanilla

In a bowl, combine crushed chocolate wafers, almonds, 1/3 cup sugar and butter. Pat the mixture onto bottom and up sides of a buttered 9 1/2" springform pan. In a large bowl, cream together cream cheese and 1 cup sugar; add eggs, one at a time, beating well after each addition. Add heavy cream, Amaretto, and vanilla and beat until light. Pour batter into shell and bake at 375 degrees for 30 minutes. Transfer to a cake rack and let stand 5 minutes. In another bowl, combine sour cream with 1 tablespoon sugar and vanilla. Spread evenly over cake and bake 5 minutes more. Transfer cake to rack to cool completely. Chill overnight.

"This is a very elegant recipe that is quite easy to make."

Sheila Ryan Kerber   **Actis Junior High School, Bakersfield, CA**

CHOCOLATE PEANUT BUTTER PIZZA

Makes 1 pizza

> 1/2 cup margarine
> 1/2 cup peanut butter
> 1 1/2 cups flour
> 1/2 cup sugar
> 1/2 cup brown sugar
> 1 egg
> 1/2 teaspoon vanilla
> 2 cups mini marshmallows
> 6 ounces chocolate chips
> 1 1/2 cups M&M candies

Mix margarine and peanut butter 30 seconds with a mixer. Add 1/2 cup flour, sugar,

133

brown sugar, egg and vanilla; mix well. Add remaining flour and mix. Press into a 12" to 14" pizza pan, forming rim around the edge. Bake at 375 degrees 8 to 10 minutes. Remove from oven and sprinkle marshmallow and chocolate chips over crust. Return to oven and bake 5 minutes. Remove and sprinkle M&M's over pizza. Allow to cool before cutting.

Jeanette Atkinson   **Brinley Middle School, Las Vegas, NV**

CHOCOLATE TORTA
Serves 8

Crust:
4 to 5 cups flour
1 teaspoon baking powder
1 to 1 ½ cups sugar
1 cube butter, melted
4 eggs, beaten
1 teaspoon vanilla
Filling:
5 ½ heaping tablespoons cornstarch
4 ½ heaping tablespoons cocoa
3 ¾ cups milk, divided
1 ¾ to 2 cups sugar, divided
1 egg, beaten
¼ cup whiskey
¼ cup rice, cooked
1 cup walnuts, finely ground
½ cup walnuts, chopped
1 cup vanilla wafers, crushed
1 teaspoon vanilla
decorator's candy

Crust: Combine dry ingredients in large bowl. Add liquid to make a very stiff dough. Roll out like pie dough. Grease two 9" pie shells. Shape dough into pie shells, letting crust hang over until filling is in place.
Filling: In a heavy saucepan, combine cornstarch and cocoa. Slowly add ¾ cup milk; mix well. Add remaining milk and 1 ¾ cup sugar; warm. Add egg and whiskey. When it starts to thicken, add rice, nuts and crushed vanilla wafers. Continue to cook until thicken. Add vanilla. Taste and add more sugar if needed. Pour filling into both pie shells. Make lattice over the filling and shape the edge. Brush with egg white and sprinkle with decorator's candy. Bake at 350 until is golden brown.

Jane Sulenta Greaves   **Central High School, Fresno, CA**

FLORENTINES
Makes 2 dozen

1 cup almonds, sliced, divided
¼ cup whipping cream
⅓ cup granulated sugar
¼ cup butter
½ cup candied orange peel, finely chopped
2 tablespoons flour
1 cup semi-sweet chocolate chips

Preheat oven to 350 degrees. Process ½ cup sliced almonds in food processor or blender until finely ground; set aside. Combine cream, sugar and butter in small saucepan. Cook, stirring occasionally over low heat until butter is melted. Turn heat to medium-high and bring to a boil. Remove from heat and add sliced almonds, ground almonds, orange peel and flour. Drop by teaspoonfuls onto lightly greased and floured cookie sheets. Spread thinly with the back of a spoon. Bake 8 to 10 minutes or until edges are golden brown. Centers will be bubbling. Let cool 2 minutes to set, then remove to a wire rack. When completely cool, turn cookies upside down on a sheet of waxed paper. Melt chocolate chips. Using a pastry brush, paint the backs of each cookie with a thin layer of chocolate. Store in covered tin.

"These are very elegant and easy cookies to make.
Candied lemon peel may be used instead of orange peel."

Doreen Lee   **Emerson Junior High School, Davis , CA**

FRESH FRUIT PIZZA
Makes Two 12" pizzas

Pizza Crust:
1 package dry yeast
¼ cup warm water (110 to 115 degrees)
½ cup milk
¼ cup shortening
1 egg, slightly beaten
2 tablespoons sugar
1 teaspoon salt
2 ½ to 3 cups flour
Glaze:
⅔ cup apple juice
2 teaspoons cornstarch
Topping:
1 (8 ounce) package cream cheese, softened
¼ cup sugar
1 teaspoon fresh lemon peel
6 cups fresh assorted fruits, sliced

Crust: Sprinkle yeast over water; set aside. In a glass bowl, place the milk and shortening and microwave on HIGH 1 to 2 minutes, until shortening melts. Let cool to warm (115 degrees). Blend in remaining ingredients except flour. Add flour, 1 cup at a time, beating with an electric mixer until too stiff. Finish by hand. Knead until smooth on a well floured surface. Lightly grease a glass bowl. Place dough inside and cover with waxed paper. Microwave 4 minutes on 10% power. Let stand 15 minutes. Repeat once or twice, until doubled in size. Punch down and press onto two greased 12" pizza pans. Shape a rounded edge, then prick crust thoroughly and bake at 400 degrees for 10 to 15 minutes until lightly browned.

Glaze: Combine apple juice with cornstarch. Microwave on HIGH 2 to 2 ½ minutes, stirring frequently, until thick and clear. Allow to cool.

Topping: Mix cream cheese with sugar and lemon peel. Spread on one crust. Arrange fruit in slices concentrically. Drizzle with glaze and refrigerate until ready.

"My family likes a combination of blueberries, strawberries,
nectarines or peaches, mandarin oranges and red and green grapes."

Joan Goodell   **Eldorado High School, Las Vegas, NV**

Fresh Orange Gelato

2 eggs + 2 egg yolks
$2/3$ cup + 2 tablespoons granulated sugar
2 cups orange juice, freshly squeezed
3 cups heavy whipping cream
juice of 2 lemons
$1/2$ teaspoon vanilla

Use an electric mixer to beat eggs, egg yolks and sugar until pale and creamy. Add the orange juice, whipping cream, lemon juice and vanilla. Blend together. Transfer mixture to an ice cream maker and freeze. If you're not using an ice cream freezer, freeze mixture in a shallow pan until almost solid, then blend in a food processor. Place mixture in freezer to finish freezing.

"I've served this following an Italian meal. The light texture and cold temperature make it the perfect complement."

Judy Henry   **Newhart Middle School, Mission Viejo, CA**

Frozen Coffee Cream Cups

Serves 10

2 egg whites
$1/2$ cup sugar
2 teaspoons instant coffee powder
1 cup whipping cream
1 teaspoon vanilla
1 drop almond extract
$1/3$ cup almonds, chopped, toasted
Garnish: Whipped cream, cherries with stems

Beat egg whites until frothy. Begin adding sugar, one tablespoon at a time; beat well after each addition. Sprinkle coffee powder over top and continue beating until stiff and satiny. In another bowl, beat cream, vanilla and almond extract until fluffy. Carefully fold whipped cream mixture into egg white mixture. Then fold in toasted almonds. Spoon into parfait glasses and top with whipped cream and a stemmed cherry for a fancy dessert. NOTE: Freezes well. Spoon into paper cups set in a muffin pan. Freeze. Remove from muffin pan and pack in airtight container for storage.

"This recipe is one of my favorites and may be made in large quantity."

Nancy Jordan   **Merced High School, Merced, CA**

Frozen Italian Pineapple Delight

1 (20 ounce) can crushed pineapple
3 eggs, separated
$1/2$ cup sugar, divided
$1/4$ teaspoon salt
4 $1/2$ teaspoons lemon juice
1 cup whipping cream, whipped
$1/4$ cup walnuts, chopped
$1/4$ cup vanilla cookie crumbs (about 12 cookies)

Early in day or up to 1 month ahead: Drain pineapple, set juice aside. In top of double boiler, with wire whisk or hand beater, beat egg yolks, all but 2 tablespoons sugar and salt until mixture is pale yellow. Gradually beat in lemon juice and reserved pineapple juice. Place double boiler top over hot, not boiling, water; cook 15 to 20 minutes, stirring, until mixture is thickened and coats spoon. Remove from heat. Stir in pineapple; cover and refrigerate. In small bowl, with mixer at high speed, beat egg whites until soft peaks form. Beating at high speed, gradually sprinkle in remaining 2 tablespoons sugar, 1 tablespoon at a time, beating until sugar is completely dissolved after each addition. (Whites should stand in stiff peaks.) Fold egg whites and whipped cream into cooled custard. Spoon ½ cup mixture into each of ten 6 ounce custard cups. In small bowl, combine walnuts and vanilla cookie crumbs. Sprinkle custard with nut mixture. Cover and freeze until firm. To Serve: Let dessert stand at room temperature about 10 minutes to soften slightly.

"Everyone likes this and the ability to prepare it early is convenient."
Carol Goddard   **Alhambra High School, Alhambra, CA**

FRUIT PIZZA
Serves 8 - 12

 1 roll Slice & Bake sugar cookies
 8 ounces cream cheese
 16 ounces Cool Whip
 fruits of your choice: kiwi, bananas, strawberries,
     blueberries, mandarin oranges, etc., sliced
 ¾ cup sugar
 2 ¼ tablespoons cornstarch
 ¾ cup orange juice
 3 tablespoons lemon juice

Slice cookie dough and place on a greased pizza pan with slices touching. Bake until slightly browned; cool. Combine cream cheese with Cool Whip; beat until smooth. Spread over cooled crust. Arrange sliced fruits over mixture. Combine sugar, cornstarch and juices in small saucepan. Bring to a boil; boil 1 minute or until thick and clear. Pour over sliced fruit. Chill before serving.

"Even non-dessert eaters love this one. Use lowfat cream cheese and Cool Whip in this."
Patty Bulat   **Rogers Middle School, Long Beach, CA**

GARLIC ICE CREAM
Serves 4 - 5

 3 cups whole milk
 ¼ teaspoon fresh garlic, chopped
 1 vanilla bean, split in half
 1 cup heavy cream
 1 ½ cups granulated sugar
 9 egg yolks

Put milk, garlic and vanilla bean in saucepan. Bring to a boil slowly, them remove from heat. In a mixing bowl, blend cream with sugar and egg yolks. Strain scalded milk mixture into egg mixture, stirring constantly. Return combined mixture to pan and stir continuously over moderate heat until it coats the back of a spoon, about 10 to 15 minutes. Cool in an ice bath. Freeze until firm.

"Straight from Gilroy and the Stinking Rose Restaurant.
This is a very unusual way to finish off an Italian dinner."
Stephanie San Sebastian   **Central High School - East, Fresno, CA**

GRANITA (LEMON ICE)

Serves 4

    2 cups water
    ¹⁄₂ cup sugar
    juice of 3 to 4 large lemons
    lemon rind twists

In a 1 quart microwaveable glass bowl, combine water and sugar; stir. Microwave, uncovered, on HIGH for 3 minutes. Stir again. Microwave on HIGH 3 to 5 minutes, until sugar is completely dissolved and water is simmering. Stir in lemon juice and let cool 15 minutes. Pour mixture into ice cube tray (without dividers) or a shallow 8" cake pan. Freeze 1 hour. Stir sides and bottom of pan with a fork to break up ice that has formed. Repeat this process every half hour for 2 or more hours, until granita has a firm, but slightly slushy consistency. To serve, scoop granita into small dessert bowls and garnish with twists of lemon rind. If not serving right away, cover and keep frozen until ready to use.

Cindy Peters   **Black Diamond Middle School, Antioch, CA**

HAZELNUT COCOA BALLS

Makes 5 dozen ³⁄₄" balls

    1 cup butter, soft
    ¹⁄₄ cup sugar
    2 tablespoons Frangelico liqueur
    ¹⁄₂ cup unsweetened cocoa
    1 ¹⁄₂ cups flour
    1 cup hazelnuts, ground
    Optional: Powdered sugar

Cream butter and sugar together with a wooden spoon. Add Frangelico, cocoa and flour. Mix well. Add hazelnuts and stir. Shape into ³⁄₄" balls. Place on greased baking sheet 1" apart. Bake at 325 degrees for 14 minutes. Cool on racks. Store in tin. *Optional:* While warm, roll in powdered sugar.

Becky Oppen   **Dana Hills High School, Dana Point, CA**

ITALIAN CAFE RUM CAKE

Serves 6 - 8

    4 eggs, separated
    6 teaspoons granulated sugar, divided
    5 tablespoons rum
    1 ¹⁄₄ cups strong Italian espresso coffee
    5 tablespoons water
    1 (16 ounce) pound cake
    10 ounces semi-sweet chocolate chips, divided
    1 teaspoon butter
    Garnish: Chocolate curls, whipped cream,
        maraschino cherries, chopped walnuts

Preheat oven to 250 degrees. Beat egg yolks together with 1 teaspoon sugar until yolks turn pale yellow. Line a 9" baking pan with buttered waxed paper, extending it up sides and above rim. Combine rum, coffee, 5 teaspoons sugar and water in small dish. Cut the pound cake into ¹⁄₄" thick slices. Dip each slice in rum/coffee mixture and place on the bottom and along sides of the baking pan, until it's completely lined with cake. (Dip slices quickly as cake will become soggy. If you run out of rum/coffee mixture, prepare more following same recipe.) Place 6 ounces chocolate chips in a small saucepan and melt, in preheated oven. Pour melted chocolate into beaten egg yolks. Whip egg whites until they form stiff peaks. Combine 1 tablespoon of beaten egg whites with the egg yolks and chocolate, mixing together; then add remaining egg whites, folding them gently into mixture. Spoon entire mixture over cake slices. Cover with more slices of pound cake dipped in rum/coffee mixture. Refrigerate overnight. The following day, turn the pan over on a flat serving platter. Carefully peel off waxed paper. Prepare frosting by melting 4 ounces of chocolate chips along with 1 teaspoon butter. Cover entire exposed surface of cake with melted chocolate. Refrigerate for 1 hour or less until chocolate hardens. Decorate with chocolate curls, whipped cream, maraschino cherries and chopped walnuts.

"Simple, but quite special. Make one day in advance, requires overnight refrigeration. Use the Italian espresso and not bland American coffee. Add whipped cream before serving."
Becky Bolt   **Bear Creek High School, Stockton, CA**

ITALIAN COOKIES
Makes 3 - 4 dozen

- $\frac{1}{2}$ cup shortening
- 1 $\frac{1}{2}$ cups sugar
- 5 eggs, (save 1 egg white for icing)
- $\frac{1}{3}$ cup wine or milk
- 1 $\frac{1}{2}$ teaspoons anise flavoring
- 4 cups flour (or more)
- 1 teaspoon baking powder
- $\frac{1}{4}$ teaspoon salt
- $\frac{3}{4}$ cup nuts, chopped
- 5 heaping tablespoons powdered sugar

Cream together shortening and sugar. Add eggs (reserving 1 egg white for frosting). Add wine or milk, and anise flavoring. Sift together flour, baking powder and salt. Add to creamed mixture; mix well. Stir in nuts. Make a 1" thick roll onto a cookie sheet. Bake a 350 degrees 18 to 20 minutes, until lightly browned. Turn oven off. Mix together egg white with powdered sugar. Pour over cookie while still hot, then slice at an angle. Return to oven to let dry.

"Friends, Sophia and Ed and I have a little contest about who makes the best anise cookies. This is Ed's since I have my grandma's recipe in another California Cookbook!"
Maria Fregulia   **Lassen High School, Susanville, CA**

When cooking pasta for casseroles, cook 3 to 5 minutes less than package directions. To conserve energy and prevent pasta from sticking together, stir pasta into boiling water to which you've added 1 tablespoon oil or margarine. Boil 3 minutes, stir, cover and remove from heat.

Mary Lash   **Paramount HS, Paramount, CA**

ITALIAN CREAM CAKE

Serves 20

nonstick cooking spray
2 cups sugar
½ cup light butter
2 (large) egg yolks
2 cups all-purpose flour
1 teaspoon baking soda
1 cup lowfat buttermilk
½ cup pecans, chopped
1 teaspoon butter extract
1 teaspoon coconut extract
1 teaspoon vanilla extract
6 (large) egg whites
lemon rind (optional)
Frosting:
1 (4 ounce) package fat free cream cheese, chilled
¼ cup butter or margarine, softened
1 teaspoon lemon rind, grated
1 teaspoon vanilla extract
3 ½ cups powdered sugar

Preheat oven to 350 degrees. Coat bottoms of three 9" round cake pans with nonstick cooking spray (do not coat sides of pans). Line bottom of pans with waxed paper. Coat waxed paper with cooking spray; dust with flour and set aside. Combine sugar and butter in large bowl; beat at medium speed until well blended. Add egg yolks, one at a time, beating well after each addition. Combine flour and baking soda; add to creamed mixture alternately with buttermilk, beginning and ending with flour mixture. Stir in pecans and extracts. Beat egg whites at high speed using clean dry beaters, until stiff peaks form (do not overbeat). Fold egg whites into batter and pour into prepared pans. Bake 23 minutes. Cool in pans 5 minutes on wire rack. Loosen layers from sides of pans using a narrow metal spatula. Turn out onto wire racks. Peel off waxed paper and cool completely.

Frosting: Beat first 4 ingredients at medium speed until smooth. Gradually add sugar to butter mixture and beat at low speed just until blended (do not overbeat).

Place 1 layer of cake on a plate. Spread with ⅔ cup frosting and top with another cake layer. Repeat two times. Spread remaining frosting over sides of cake. Garnish with lemon rind, if desired. Store cake in refrigerator and bring to room temperature before serving. NOTE: Light butter is okay to use for baking.

"Our family's favorite. Good with ice cream (which lessens the light benefits, of course!)."
Wendy Johnson   **Temecula Valley High School, Temecula, CA**

---

*Florentine cookies were originally created in Florence,
Italy during the 15th or 16th century.*

Doreen Lee   **Emerson JHS, Davis, CA**

ITALIAN NUT ROLL

Makes 24

1 ½ sticks margarine, softened
3 cups flour
3 eggs, separated
2 ½ tablespoons sour cream
1 teaspoon salt
2 teaspoons vanilla
1 cup sugar
1 pound nuts, chopped
powdered sugar, for topping

Combine margarine and flour in bowl; blend together. (Separate eggs and chill egg whites for use later.) Add egg yolks and sour cream to flour mixture, blending well. Blend in salt and 1 teaspoon vanilla. Knead into ball; chill overnight. Next day, let dough stand at room temperature. Preheat oven to 350 degrees. In medium sized bowl, beat egg whites until soft peaks form. Add sugar and beat until stiff. Stir in remaining 1 teaspoon vanilla and chopped nuts; beat well; set aside. Using rolling pin, roll dough to ¼" thickness; cut into squares or circles. Place 1 teaspoon nut filling on each cookie square or circle. Roll into logs and place on cookie sheet; bake until light brown. Remove from pan and roll in powdered sugar while still hot.

Nancy Patten   **Placerita Junior High School, Newhall, CA**

ITALIAN SPICE COOKIES

Makes 27 dozen

Cookies:
1 (15 ounce) box raisins
4 pounds flour
2 ½ pounds sugar
4 heaping tablespoons baking powder
1 tablespoon pepper
1 tablespoon cinnamon
1 tablespoon ground cloves
2 oranges and their juice
2 orange rinds, finely grated
8 ounces cocoa
1 pound shortening
1 cup walnuts, chopped
Glaze:
2 pounds powdered sugar
water

Cookies: Place raisins in a bowl and cover with warm water to soak. Drain, reserve water. Using a very large bowl, mix together all ingredients by hand, adding raisin water until bread dough consistency is reached. Knead dough. Roll sections into long 1" thick rolls. Cut into 1" pieces with knife. Shape into balls. Place on ungreased cookie sheet. Bake at 400 degrees 5 minutes on lower rack and 5 minutes on upper rack. Remove and cool on wire rack. Cookies will be soft.
Glaze: Combine powdered sugar with enough water added to reach a medium-thick consistency. Roll each cookie in glaze and dry on wire rack.

"From a Polish friend in New York. I always have someone help make it at Christmas."
Julia Lane   **Eldorado High School, Las Vegas, NV**

Italian Trifle
Serves 6

1 sponge cake
¼ cup Amaretto di Saronno
⅓ cup tart currant jam
4 egg yolks
¼ cup sugar
pinch salt
2 cups scalded milk
1 teaspoon vanilla
1 cup sweetened whipped cream

Line a glass bowl with 1" thick layer of sponge cake. Moisten with Amaretto and spread thinly with jam. Beat egg yolks lightly in the top of a double-boiler. Stir in sugar and salt and gradually add milk. Cook, stirring constantly, until mixture begins to thicken. Remove from heat, add vanilla, then chill, stirring occasionally. Pour over cake and top with whipped cream.

"I found this in a booklet produced by Amaretto di Saronno to promote their liqueur."
Pat Dallas   **Westminster High School, Westminster, CA**

Mocha Cream Cannoli
Serves 6

1 cup heavy cream
1 tablespoon instant coffee
¼ cup powdered sugar
½ cup miniature semi-sweet chocolate chips
6 cannoli shells (3 ounce package)

Beat heavy cream, instant coffee and powdered sugar until stiff peaks form. Fold in miniature chips. Just before serving fill cannoli shells with cream using a piping bag or knife, so they don't become soggy.

"Mocha cream is also delicious served over slices of chocolate or angel food cake."
Nan Paul   **Grant Middle School, Escondido, CA**

Sherry Cake
Serves 10 - 12

1 package yellow cake mix (no pudding)
1 (small) package vanilla instant pudding
¾ cup cream sherry
1 tablespoon Grand Marnier
4 eggs
dash cinnamon
¾ cup vegetable oil
powdered sugar, for dusting

Mix dry ingredients together. Add remaining ingredients and mix with electric mixer on low speed for 5 minutes. Bake in ungreased bundt pan or tube pan at 340 degrees for 50 to 60 minutes. Cool in pan, upright, for 20 minutes. Remove cake from pan and dust with powdered sugar.

"This is a great dessert that finishes up any Italian meal perfectly.
Very moist and a great complement for an espresso or cappuccino."
Deanna Lee   **Marina High School, Huntington Beach, CA**

SICILIAN CHOCOLATE CAKE

Serves 6 - 8

Cake:
1 9" x 3" pound cake
1 pound ricotta cheese
2 tablespoons heavy cream
$1/4$ cup sugar
3 tablespoons orange-flavored liqueur
3 tablespoons candied fruit, coarsely chopped
2 ounces semi-sweet chocolate pieces

Frosting:
12 ounces semi-sweet chocolate chips
$3/4$ cup strong black coffee
$1/2$ pound unsalted butter, cut into $1/2$" pieces, thoroughly chilled

Cake: With a sharp, serrated knife, slice the end crusts off pound cake and level the top if it's rounded. Cut the cake horizontally into $1/2$" to $3/4$" slices. Rub the ricotta cheese through a coarse sieve with a wooden spoon into a bowl; beat until smooth. Beating constantly, add the cream, sugar and liqueur. Fold in chopped fruit and chocolate pieces. Center the bottom slab of cake on serving platter and spread generously with ricotta mix. Add another slab and spread with more ricotta. Repeat until all the cake slabs are reassembled and filling is used up, ending with cake slice on top. Gently press loaf together to make it as compact as possible. (Don't worry if it's wobbly; chilling firms the loaf.) Refrigerate cake for 2 hours, or until firm.
Frosting: Melt chocolate with coffee in a saucepan over low heat, stirring constantly until chocolate has completely dissolved. Remove pan from heat and beat in chilled butter, one piece at a time. Continue beating until mixture is smooth. Chill the frosting until it's spreading consistency. Spread frosting evenly over top and sides of chilled cake. Cover with waxed paper, plastic wrap or aluminum foil and let cake "ripen" in refrigerator at least 24 hours before serving.

"This is a great cake to make ahead and refrigerate."

Debby Truitt　　　　　　　　　**Woodland High School, Woodland, CA**

SPUMONI ICE CREAM CUPS

Serves 10

1 quart vanilla ice cream
$1/2$ cup slivered almonds, toasted
1 (1.75 ounce) milk chocolate bar
$1/4$ cup red and green maraschino cherries
$1/4$ teaspoon orange peel, grated
$1/4$ teaspoon lemon peel, grated

In a large bowl, stir ice cream to soften slightly. Stir and blend in remaining ingredients. Line muffin pan with 10 paper baking cups. Spoon ice cream mixture into paper cups. Freeze until firm.

"For a final touch, top with whipped cream before serving."

Joanne Fial　　　　　　　　　**East Middle School, Downey, CA**

STUFFED PEARS MILANESE STYLE
Serves 6

½ cup almonds, chopped
1 tablespoon butter
1 (20 ounce) can pear halves
½ cup sugar
¼ teaspoon almond extract
6 maraschino cherries, chopped
½ cup sweet white wine

Combine almonds with butter in a small cup; toast in microwave, stirring occasionally, until light brown. Drain pear halves and arrange in a circular dish with the large ends of pears around outer edge of container. Mix almonds, sugar, almond extract and cherries. Spoon into pear cavities. Pour 1 teaspoon wine into each pear cavity, then pour remaining wine in dish. Bake, covered, in microwave on HIGH for 4 minutes. Pears can be served hot or cold.

"This is a light finish dessert to a rich Italian dinner."

Stephanie San Sebastian   **Central High School, Fresno, CA**

TIRAMISU TOFFEE TORTE
Serves 8 - 12   *Photo opposite page 129*

Cake:
1 (1 pound 2.5 ounce) package white cake mix with pudding
1 cup strong coffee, room temperature
4 egg whites
4 (1.4 ounce) toffee candy bars, finely chopped
Frosting:
⅔ cup sugar
⅓ cup chocolate syrup
½ (8 ounce) package cream cheese, softened
2 cups whipping cream
2 teaspoons vanilla
1 cup strong coffee, room temperature, divided
Garnish: Toffee candy bars, chopped or chocolate curls, if desired

Cake: Heat oven to 350 degrees. Grease and flour two 8" or 9" round cake pans. In large bowl, combine cake mix, 1 cup coffee and egg whites at low speed until moistened; beat 2 minutes at high speed. Fold in chopped toffee bars. Spread batter into prepared pans. Bake 8" pans 30 to 40 minutes; bake 9" pans 20 to 30 minutes; until toothpick inserted in center comes out clean. Cool 10 minutes; remove from pan and cool completely.

Frosting: In medium bowl, combine sugar, chocolate syrup and cream cheese; beat until smooth. Add whipping cream and vanilla; beat until light and fluffy. Refrigerate until ready to use.

To assemble cake: Slice each layer in half horizontally to make 4 layers. Drizzle each cut side with ¼ cup coffee. Place 1 layer, coffee side up, on serving plate; spread with ¾ cup frosting. Repeat with second and third cake layers. Top with remaining cake layer and frost. Garnish as desired.

Pillsbury Company   **Minnesota, MN**

TIRAMISU
Serves 6

1 cup whipping cream
8 ounces cream cheese, room temperature
$\frac{1}{2}$ cup powdered sugar
1 teaspoon vanilla
$\frac{1}{2}$ cup cold espresso or strong coffee
1 package ladyfingers (12)
1 Hershey's chocolate bar, shaved into curls

In electric mixer, whip cream until stiff; remove from bowl and set aside. In same mixing bowl (no need to clean it), whip cream cheese until smooth, then add powdered sugar, vanilla and 2 tablespoons of the espresso. Fold whipped cream and cream cheese mixture together. Arrange ladyfinger halves in the bottom of an 8" baking dish. Sprinkle half of the remaining cold espresso over ladyfingers. Spoon half of the cream cheese/whipped cream mixture on top. Repeat. Top with chocolate curls, made from chocolate bar.

"In our school catering business, we tested several recipes for tiramisu. This was the best!"

Kit Little   **Foothill High School, Pleasanton, CA**

TORTONI
Serves 6 - 8

$\frac{1}{2}$ cup sugar
2 tablespoons cornstarch
$\frac{1}{8}$ teaspoon salt
2 cups milk
2 egg yolks, slightly beaten
2 tablespoons butter
2 teaspoons vanilla
$\frac{1}{2}$ cup light Karo syrup
$\frac{1}{2}$ teaspoon almond extract
1 cup whipping cream
$\frac{1}{2}$ cup nuts, chopped (optional)

Mix sugar, cornstarch and salt in saucepan; stir in milk gradually. Cook and stir over medium heat until mixture thickens and boils. Boil and stir 1 minute. Stir at least half of the hot mixture gradually into the egg yolks, Return it to saucepan and boil and stir 1 minute. Remove from heat and stir in butter and vanilla. Stir in Karo syrup and almond extract. Chill in saucepan with waxed paper on top (can be put in freezer to speed up cooling). Beat whipping cream until stiff peaks form. Fold into cooled pudding. Pour into an 8" x 8" pan and top with chopped nuts. Freeze.

Charlotte Runyan   **Saddleback High School, Santa Ana, CA**

WHITE CHOCOLATE MACADAMIA BISCOTTI

Makes 3 1/2 to 4 dozen

- 1/2 cup butter
- 3/4 cup sugar
- 2 eggs
- 1 teaspoon vanilla
- 2 tablespoons Amaretto liqueur
- 2 cups + 2 tablespoons all-purpose flour, divided
- 1 1/2 teaspoons baking powder
- 1/4 teaspoon salt
- 2/3 cups macadamia nuts, chopped
- 2/3 cup white chocolate chips

Preheat oven to 325 degrees. In a mixing bowl, cream butter and sugar until light and fluffy. Beat in eggs, vanilla and Amaretto. In a separate bowl, combine 2 cups flour, baking powder and salt. Add to creamed mixture, blending well. Fold in nuts and chocolate chips, Divide dough in half. On a greased and floured baking sheet, pat out dough into 2 logs about 1/2" high, 1 1/2" wide and 14" long, spacing them at least 2" apart. Bake in the middle of oven for 25 minutes, or until lightly browned. Transfer from baking sheet to rack. Cool 5 minutes. Place on a cutting board and using a serrated knife, slice diagonally on a 45 degree angle about 1/2" thick. Place slices upright on the baking sheet and return to oven for about 8 minutes longer to dry slightly. Let cool on a rack. Store in tightly covered container.

Betty Rabin   **Sierra Vista Junior High School, Canyon Country, CA**

Cut fat and calories in creamy sauces by substituting evaporated skim milk for cream in your favorite recipes.

Patty Bulat   **Rogers MS, Long Beach, CA**

We gratefully acknowledge our
Contributors

Easy Italian Favorites

Contributors

Easy Italian Favorites

R

S

Easy Italian Favorites

Easy Italian Favorites

Breads & Pasta

Sauces

Pizza

Chicken

Easy Italian Favorites

Pork

Seafood

Meatless

Desserts

Easy Italian Favorites

1907 Skycrest Drive
Fullerton, CA 92831

Please send me _____ copy(s) of Easy Italian Favorites at $9.95ea. (includes tax and postage).
Make checks payable to California Cookbook Company.

Enclosed is my check for _____ book(s) at $9.95 ea $_____.

Name _____

Address _____

City _____ State _____ Zip _____

1907 Skycrest Drive
Fullerton, CA 92831

Please send me _____ copy(s) of Easy Italian Favorites at $9.95ea. (includes tax and postage).
Make checks payable to California Cookbook Company.

Enclosed is my check for _____ book(s) at $9.95 ea $_____.

Name _____

Address _____

City _____ State _____ Zip _____

1907 Skycrest Drive
Fullerton, CA 92831

Please send me _____ copy(s) of Easy Italian Favorites at $9.95ea. (includes tax and postage).
Make checks payable to California Cookbook Company.

Enclosed is my check for _____ book(s) at $9.95 ea $_____.

Name _____

Address _____

City _____ State _____ Zip _____

Easy Italian Favorites